THE WELL-MANNERED

HORSE

DEVELOPING AN IDEAL EQUINE BUDDY

MEREDITH HILL

ISBN: 978-1-953714-65-7

DOWNLOAD YOUR FREE CHECKLIST NOW!

If you've ever checked out an equine supply website or stopped by a tack shop, you might find your head swimming regarding all of the stuff people buy to help them care for their horses. How do you decide what you need to buy? I've created this checklist to help new horse owners get organized right from the start.

Go to **https://free.meredithhillbook.com/checklist** or scan this code

to download it for free

ALSO BY MEREDITH HILL

Before Your Horse Comes Home

Finding Your First Horse

I Have A Horse... Now What?

Why Does My Horse Act like this?

CONTENTS

INTRODUCTION

Ah, horses. Many of us are captivated by the beauty and grace of these majestic creatures. Horses are blessed with a natural elegance, and watching one gallop around evokes feelings of freedom, strength, and majesty. Yet, underneath the glossy coats, velvety muzzles, and large expressive eyes are a myriad of opinions and instincts—not all of which align readily with the opinions and instincts of their human counterparts.

Furthermore, horses are large, wily animals. They're tall, muscular, and well-equipped with hooves that can kick and teeth that can bite. As big, fast prey animals, they know a lot of ways to get away from objects and situations that they don't like or trust. And, while many of us on the human side of the discussion consider ourselves strong or fast, we are not horse strong or horse fast.

You've probably heard of the term "horsepower" when referring to vehicles, but have you ever wondered what "horsepower" really means? The term was coined by James Watt–the same guy after whom the measure of power is named. In the 1700s, Watt was attempting to compare the power of his newly re-engineered steam engine to the capability of the horses who might be replaced by the engine. He observed horses working to turn a mill wheel and determined that they turned the wheel 2.5 times per minute. Using the definition of "work" as energy transferred over a period of time, he calculated that one horsepower equals 33,000 foot-pounds of work per minute. You can think of this also as the power needed to lift an object that weighs 33,000 pounds one foot above the ground in one minute.

Modern calculations indicate that today's horses have an average of 15 horsepower. Humans, on the other hand, aren't quite as powerful. It's estimated that a very athletic human is capable of approximately 1.2 horsepower.

Physics and math are fascinating and all, but you're probably wondering what this has to do with horses and manners. My point is simple: you cannot win a tug-of-war match with a horse. It's simply not possible, given the rules of physics. You cannot run faster than they do or jump higher than they can, and with all of their hard-wired, finely-tuned instincts, it's not likely that you'll outwit them when they go into survival mode.

I recently wrote about how horses' instincts influence their behavior in my book *Why Does My Horse Act Like This: Understanding Equine Behavior in your New Horse*. In that book, we examine how horses are biologically prepared to survive and how their instincts can dictate their behavior. Some of the bad habits our horses display today are directly related to how they have evolved to stay alive in the wild.

So we've got this 15 horsepower critter with centuries of instincts, weighing in at approximately 1,000 pounds, and who is capable of speeds up to 40-50 miles per hour in one corner. In the other corner, a human. Two legs, flexible hands, 20 miles per hour on a good day. The goal is to create a partnership between the two, in which each party understands what the other is asking. What can we do to ensure the best possible rate of survival for the small, slow human?

This is where the well-mannered horse comes into the story. A horse who understands how its behavior impacts everything around it is still dangerous and unpredictable. However, a horse who understands its surroundings and other living beings, and has been taught how to behave safely, is less likely to create a dangerous situation.

They say that everyone has some sort of very strong, soul-crushing fear. Whether it can be categorically considered a phobia or not, nearly everyone has something about which they are irrationally fearful. For some, it's a fear of something that could be dangerous, like heights or swimming in the ocean. For others, it's something we can't explain, such as a fear of clowns or the number thirteen. I don't want to trigger anyone, so we won't go any further than that.

Instead, I want you to think of the way your strongest aversion makes you feel, and apply that to your horse. While we don't scientifically know exactly how horses feel when their prey instincts kick in, I like to assume that it's a deep, illogical aversion or fear that starts somewhere in their very DNA. I can identify with that feeling, and it helps me appreciate what might be running through a horse's mind and body when it's faced with something new and potentially dangerous.

What we hope to accomplish, by teaching a horse good manners, is instilling that same inner voice that tells us that while our fear might be real, the situation is not nearly as dangerous as we think it is. If we can convince ourselves not to have a meltdown when we encounter something terrifying, surely we can help our horses understand that being afraid isn't always a call to action. We've learned how to observe, analyze, and act accordingly. Teaching our horses the same is safer for us and better for them in the long run.

But there are a few cracks in this plan. First of all, horses don't exactly speak human languages. They communicate through body language, breath, nickers, whinnies, and snorts. Then there's that size difference thing again. How are we supposed to sit down and explain plastic bags to our horses in an empathetic yet assertive manner?

Instilling good manners in your horse is not an easy task, but it is incredibly important, for your safety and for the safety of anyone–or anything–that may come in contact with your horse. You need to be able to harness the 15 horsepower that lives on four legs in order to keep risk to a minimum.

In this book, we'll continue to build on knowledge of equine needs, behaviors, and instincts with an introduction to good manners, and what is considered a "well-mannered horse." We'll look at what we can reasonably expect from our horses and some of the ways we can help our horses understand what we're asking.

I don't claim to have all the answers, and reading this book will not elevate you to Big Name Trainer status overnight. What I hope to do is provide you with a few suggestions so you can evaluate and address your horse's manners in a way that is safe and practical for you and your horse.

That might mean involving a trainer or equine professional who can help you establish and maintain good behavior. To that end, I've included a discussion regarding the huge grey area surrounding appropriate training methods, and the equally concerning boundaries between reinforcement and abuse. I've learned from my readers' emails that you are very concerned about equine well-being, and worried about certain training methods. That's why we'll take a look at some of the realities of horse training to prepare you for selecting a professional to assist you, should you choose to go that route.

I wish I had the magical power to make a wish and grant everyone who reads this a well-mannered horse. In fact, I wish I had the magical power to make my own fuzzy beasts behave 100% of the time. Instead, I have worked with them for years and will continue to work with them to help them make the best decisions they can when strange things happen. Still, they are living beings, and occasionally, they make decisions that defy human logic.

We'll take a glance at how to work with certain behavioral issues as we touch on them. I want you to keep in mind, though, that there is no one absolute, fail-proof way to train a horse to do or not do something. Just as people learn in different ways, each horse will respond to different "asks" –or training requests that we make– in different ways. I very much do not want anyone to get hurt or do something that is outside of their comfort zone or realm of knowledge. That can make matters even worse.

Instead, know that working with a professional is a great option for those times when your horse's issues are beyond your training ability. Honesty and humility are important qualities to practice when working with beings as large and powerful as horses. If you are "overhorsed," as we call it, you may make decisions based on your own danger instincts. Instead of trying to suffer through this type of situation, it's a smart idea to contact a professional.

Of course, there are plenty of questionable professionals in this world. To help you navigate the world of equine professionals such as trainers, behaviorists, and handlers, I've included a brief discussion regarding some of the many training debates that persist in the equine world. My goal is not to persuade you to take a side, or to change your mind. I simply wish to present all perspectives, as well as common arguments for and against each approach. Therefore, don't think of this book as an endorsement for any particular training method or approach–it's just your horse buddy Meredith telling you about some of the things you might want to think about when considering training for your horse.

Let's start by looking at how good manners are defined so you have a clearer idea of what you should expect from your equine companion. We'll then observe and analyze what your hooved beast is currently doing to determine the best way to get on the same page. As with each of my books, a Resources section will round things up with websites where you can learn more about many of the topics discussed.

With all that said, get ready to dive into what makes an equine good citizen, and how a horse or pony earns such a designation!

SECTION 1: WHAT ARE EQUINE GOOD MANNERS?

When we think of "good manners," we think of things like saying "please" and "thank you," or actions such as holding a door open for a person who has their hands full. We do not (and should not) expect these types of manners from horses. They don't have the linguistic capability to speak English, and they lack thumbs, so operating doorknobs is a challenge for them.

For the most part, equine good manners boil down to acting in a rational, minimally dangerous manner. There are different ways in which they can demonstrate this preferred behavior, as well. When a horse generally manages to exist peacefully in a stall without damaging itself or the barn, we say that they have "good stall manners." When a horse is being handled by someone, such as being led down the barn aisleway, groomed, or tacked up, without incident, we say that the horse has "good ground manners". When you are able to take your horse into situations where they may encounter other horses, dogs, humans, children, unfamiliar objects, plastic bags, or a ringtone they may not have heard before, and no one cries, we say a horse is "easy to handle."

When a horse is difficult to handle, there is often a combination of factors at play. In most cases, the horse has simply not been desensitized to a particular object or situation. As far as they're concerned, that wheelbarrow in a different place is a horse-eating monster, and that didgeridoo ringtone is the beckoning of the end of days. They have no basis for understanding what it is, they think it's terrifying, and the appropriate reaction is fight or flight.

In addition to being afraid, a horse that demonstrates bad manners and makes choices that are less than satisfactory frequently isn't sure about boundaries or who to trust. Horses either are the leader, or they're desperately looking for the leader so they don't have to make their own decisions. If at all possible, we want the human to be the leader. But, in order for the horse to agree with that decision, they need to know that the leader is competent. In turn, this trust requires communication and understanding, so it's not just as simple as telling a horse what you want it to do in most cases. Think of it more as providing a full persuasive essay, acknowledging the pros and cons of each potential decision, delivered in a language you do not speak fluently.

There may also be some trauma in your horse's past that influences their behavior. Accidents happen, even in the kindest and most compassionate barns. As a result, your horse may be genuinely triggered by certain things.

In order to prevent them from becoming a danger to themselves and everything around them, it's critical for a horse to have at least semi-half-way-kinda decent manners I frequently draw comparisons between horses and toddlers because they're on the same wavelength, at least in my experience. They can do things that are compassionate, rational, and demonstrate advanced problem solving skills. They can also immediately about-face and have an emotional meltdown about something that you would personally categorize as insignificant.

For example, returning readers are likely familiar with my thoroughbred gelding, Red and quarter horse mare, Belle. Red made a horrible racehorse and a less-than-ideal children's horse, but over time, we've built a fantastic relationship. He's served as a therapy horse for dozens of humans and horses alike. However, he is still very much a horse. I have seen him stand perfectly still while a small child has a tantrum at his feet, but I have also watched him throw his own tantrum because he didn't want to cross a small mud puddle in his favorite pasture.

Toddlers and horses have a similar capacity for understanding what it means to have good manners, too. They may not completely understand the whys and wherefores, but they grasp the idea that if you tell them it's ok to do something, it's probably ok. They also understand what "no" means, and they'll cheerfully use it in response to your requests, too. Toddlers and horses also have a proclivity towards honesty even, and sometimes especially, when you don't necessarily want them to be quite so upfront. Red used to pin his ears at a vet he didn't like very much, and while I understood, I really wished he would be a little better at concealing his opinions!

You may be wondering whether your horse falls more into the category of "naughty" or "nice" when it comes to manners. Most horses are a combination of both, so don't feel bad if you can think of some "yes, but…" scenarios involving a time your horse was particularly heinous.

That happens to even the most staunchly obedient equine citizens, so fear not. "Generally nice" is often a good target for most horses, though we can always aim higher and work towards improvement.

Let's take a look at some of the more common situations in which a horse's manners are most important, for the sake of everyone–and everything–around them.

Chapter 1: Stall Manners

You may have also heard of stall manners as "stable manners" or "barn behavior." Each of these terms are used to describe how a horse acts when it's indoors. Though "stall," "stable," and "barn" are all specific types of structures, these terms are often used interchangeably. Regardless of the semantics, stable manners refer to how a horse behaves in regards to its surroundings indoors.

To determine whether your horse is a good citizen or a borderline hooligan, as yourself a few questions about your horse's general behavior. When locked in a stall, do they stand there patiently, or whinny and pace inconsolably? When other horses walk past the stall, does your horse bite at the walls and pin their ears, or have no noticeable reaction? When it's time to clean your horse's stall, do they casually sniff your hair or take a nap in the corner, or do they require a three-person moving team to safely transport them to another stall or paddock?

Your horse may also exhibit one of many inappropriate stall behaviors. We reviewed these topics in detail in my book *Why Does My Horse Act*

Like This: Understanding Equine Behavior in your New Horse, so I don't want to become too repetitive, but some horses have developed bad habits as a reaction to stress, pain, or behavioral issues. Horses who crib, chew, weave, stall walk, and dig aren't necessarily being ill-mannered in their destruction of property and acts of self-endangerment, but these behaviors are often categorized as bad manners. They are not encouraged, and it's best to dig deep to discover why your horse continues to do these things so that you can help them break these habits.

In our ideal human mind, a horse would stand in its stall as long as we needed them to. They would cleverly deposit waste in a corner that's easy to reach. They would ring a bell when their water bucket needed attention, and they would never, ever poo in their buckets just moments after we finished scrubbing and refilling them. They would keep their hay neatly piled, and put a tidy stack of the bits they didn't want to eat next to the door for easy disposal. They'd whinny happily at all of their neighbors, wait patiently for feeding time, and would never chew on anything, kick at the walls, or drag things from the aisleway into their stalls to destroy.

Our ideal human mind, however, has nothing to do with the instincts and capabilities of modern horses. Horses wander around in their stalls, tracking their waste wherever they go. They slobber up a mess in their water buckets, throw hay everywhere, and more or less give the place the full "rock star trashes a hotel room," treatment. Can a horse be neat and tidy and mild-mannered when locked in a stall full time? Sure. Just don't expect it.

In your ideal human mind, a horse standing in a stall is no big deal. Heck, you'd probably love to have nothing better to do than stand in a box and eat all day. On the surface, it sounds like a pretty good gig. But try to reverse your perspective and think about it from the point of view of a horse.

Yes, your horse stands there all day and does nothing but eat. But running through their fuzzy head are instincts that tell them to move more, eat more, and socialize more. Horses are genetically predisposed to roam in herds, live in the company of their friends and family, and eat constantly. The biology of horses is such that they need mental stimulation, physical exercise, and an unbelievable amount of roughage to keep them happy.

Stall manners can be taught, and bad stall habits can be curbed, but you'll want to start with a happy horse. Just as a toddler isn't particularly interested in learning about the alphabet when they've just been denied their favorite sweet, a horse who is unhappily fighting his instincts for movement and grazing isn't going to be super receptive to new information. If your horse is currently battling ulcers, they may not be interested in what you have to say about not kicking the door every time their nemesis walks down the aisleway. Obviously, if you are in an emergency situation, that goes out the window, but timing is key when it comes to modifying equine behavior.

Everyone has their own unique version of what they consider good stall manners, because everyone's barn situation is a little different. For example, if you don't have stalls, but rather a large communal run-in, you would probably like it if you could walk outside, approach your horse, and put a halter on them. If you have your horse in a traditional stall, you might find it pretty satisfactory if anyone could walk into your horse's stall to clean, feed, check the water bucket, and make sure your horse is doing well. In some barns, it's customary to groom and tack up your horse in their stall, which means you'd probably love it even more if your horse would stand still and not try to escape the stall when the door is open.

Before you start coming up with a training or discipline plan to work all the weird barn habits out of your horse, pause for a moment and prioritize. Many of us have an innate urge to correct bad behavior *right now, no exceptions!* There may be an extra sense of urgency if you are boarding your horse at another person's property because your horse is being a pest and/or dangerous and/or destructive. Now you're worried about your horse causing problems as well as being held liable for damages, and to top it all off, you might get kicked out of your barn if what your horse did was totally egregious!

No one wants to be the parent of the child lying on the floor screaming their head off in the local supermarket during peak hours. Similarly, no one wants to be the person whose horse ate the entire fence or the person whose horse dragged all of the freshly washed blankets into the stall and covered them in manure. Getting a call from a barn manager or owner informing me that my horse has been naughty is an incredibly embarrassing experience–trust me! I once had a horse who managed to do something fascinating on a near-weekly basis. Each time I got a call, I wanted to sell the horse, hide under a rock, and not think about anything horse-related, no matter how tangential.

Do not do this. Unless you have been strategically planning for some time to sell your horse and turn into a hermit, it is far simpler to apologize, take pictures of everything, document what happened, pay for anything that is legally your responsibility, and work with your horse to help them make better choices. While that does feel like a lot, selling a horse with a reputation for poor stable manners is in itself an extraordinary feat And that's *before* finding the right mountain or deep cave to hide from society for the rest of your life. So skip the real estate hunt. Stay calm. Stay rational. Take care of the horse.

Instead of fleeing town in the dead of night, it's time to start paying very close attention to everything your horse does– the good, the bad, and the inexplicable. Compare what they actually do to what you want and need them to do. Consider how they act when you:

- Enter their stall
- Approach them from a variety of angles
- Move their water bucket or attempt to fill it with a hose
- Attempt to put a halter on in their stall
- Enter with food
- Walk past their stall with and without another horse
- Stick your fingers in their stall (this is especially important if you are boarding at a facility where children are present)
- Stand outside their stall and talk to someone
- Bring a pitchfork and muck bucket into their stall while they're in it

If you have never noticed anything unusual when doing these things with your horse, then you can rest assured that your horse already has pretty good stall manners. But, if your horse becomes aggressive or agitated when these things happen, you might have a few concerns to address.

Before we get to next steps, though, let's continue to look at all of the interesting ways in which horses can choose to misbehave!

Chapter 2: When You Handle Your Horse

When you're spending time with your horse, what are you typically doing? Many of us "old-timers" go into a bit of a fugue state and have to really stop to consider the actual actions we take when we're at the barn.

If I really think about it, my pattern typically looks something like this:

- Walk up to Red or Belle's stall
- Greet them
- Grab their halter from the front of the stall
- Enter the stall and shut (but don't lock) the door behind me
- Say mushy things about how cute they are and how much I love them
- Put their halter on
- Lead them out of their stall by their halter to the cross ties (don't do this–a lead rope is a much safer and effective way to lead your horse)
- Clip the cross ties onto the halter rings
- Wander into the tack room and pull out my saddle, pads, girth, bridle, and helmet, which I stack on a rack in the aisleway piece by piece as I find them in the crowded tack room
- Groom the horse, including a good curry, body brushing, and hoof picking
- Tack them up, probably very slowly because I enjoy having time to talk to the other folks in my barn

- Walk the horse back down the aisle, past their stall, into the arena
- Fidget and fuss with the girth, stirrup leathers, saddle position, helmet straps, and gloves
- Mount up
- Make final equipment adjustments
- *Finally* start working

It's entirely forgivable if you stopped really absorbing the steps midway through, because it gets boring. I understand why my horses zone out while I'm getting ready for our rides. They have to stand patiently for a significant amount of time, doing absolutely nothing while I'm completely absorbed in my own tasks.

My Quarter Horse mare, Belle, stands completely still through the whole process because that's how she was trained as a youngster. Red, on the other hand, will fidget. As a former racehorse, he wasn't taught much about standing still for anything–many times, track horses are groomed long before a race, then saddled up on the move so they can keep their muscles warmed up for the burst of speed needed for a race.

When Red first came into my life, he lived at a barn where there were no crossties. Horses were either tacked up in stalls or ground-tied next to the area where we kept our equipment (it wasn't so much a "tack room" as a "tack space"). So, we worked at it for a while, and Red learned to ground tie rather nicely. Next, I worked on getting him to continue ground tying even when I started to pull out exciting things like saddle pads and girths. Eventually, we got a pretty good routine down, but I've never been able to convince him to stand completely still, like Belle does. He has arthritis, after all, and as a fellow sufferer, I can't imagine standing still feels very good to him. So I let him move a bit, shift his weight, and get comfortable while I talk to my trainer about something completely irrelevant for far too long.

I have, however, taught him words like "scootch," which means take a step sideways, "bootch," which is his cue to move his hindquarters away from me, "step," which is a request to take a step forward, and "back," which is a step backwards. If his wiggling positions him at an angle I don't appreciate, I can easily guide him back to where I need him with a few cues.

Assessing your horse's barn manners means seriously considering how you need your horse to behave indoors. Deciding whether or not your horse is well mannered when you handle them depends on what you ask them to do, and how much time and effort it takes to get the desired result.

Ask yourself:
- Can I easily catch my horse? Can I just walk up to them wherever they are and put their halter and leadrope on their head?
- When I try to lead my horse out of their stall/pasture, how much resistance do they give me?
- How hard do I need to work to get my horse to walk shoulder-to-shoulder with me? Do I have to drag them behind me, or am I running to catch up?
- When I'm leading my horse, how many feet do they typically have on the ground at any given time? Do I need a spotter to clear a path in front of or behind me?

- What's the most exciting thing that has happened to us while grooming or tacking up? Was it my horse's fault?
- Do people try very hard to not share an arena when I'm working my horse?
- If I had to answer the phone or go to the bathroom urgently while tacking up my horse, would there be imminent danger?
- Are people actively afraid of my horse?
- Am I actively afraid of my horse?

A horse with bad ground manners is scary and dangerous. Whether your horse is being simply contrary or is truly in some stage of "fight or flight" whenever you interact with them, there are too many things that can go wrong to allow this behavior to continue. As a responsible horse owner, you want to be able to interact with your horse safely every time. Accidents will happen, of course, but a horse who knows how to make good choices will often be better prepared to deal with mishaps.

Red is another great example of this. While racehorses aren't necessarily taught to tie while they're on the track, they are exposed to a truly mind-blowing array of traditionally scary things. People are often going in and out of their stalls at strange times. They do something different every day when they go to work. They see a seemingly endless parade of strange faces and places as they travel from track to track. A new wheelbarrow parked in the aisleway for the first time is nothing. A tractor rolling by while you're working? What–are they supposed to yield to you? Goats? They make great buddies! A lot of former racehorses take a lot in stride because they've likely seen it at the track.

Of course, that's not to say that only racehorses can be unbothered by their surroundings, or that all former racehorses are unflappable. All horses spook, but they all have different triggers, and it's important to know what is and is not a problem to them. Red demonstrated this to me early in our relationship.

While he was dancing and prancing up the aisleway during one of our tacking up training sessions, he managed to get one leg inside the wheelbarrow, and the other on the wrong side of the handles. Instead of freaking out like I fully expected him to, he paused and calmly extracted himself from the wheelbarrow. Once he had all of his feet on the ground, he shook himself and walked up to me as if to ask, "Hey, did you see that? Pretty smooth, eh?"

A few years later, I worked nearly every day for several months to encourage this same mellow creature to walk across a small creek that crossed the trail system at the barn. By "small creek," I mean that I could stand comfortably with my left foot on one bank and my right foot on the other. It was frequently dry, and rarely resembled much more than a puddle. I was never able to convince him to walk across. Not once. He would stand stock still on one side, or occasionally put his front feet in the creek, but he would not cross. As an added bonus, once he decided he'd had enough of this nonsense, he would bolt suddenly and take himself back to his stall at a dead gallop. I gave up.

As it turns out, I have never actually needed to walk Red through water, but I have led him up and down crowded aisleways, through busy barns, alongside roads, and past a variety of strange objects that he's never seen before. His original trainer taught him some very important stuff by making sure he was aware of different objects that might show up in a barn, like wheelbarrows.

Make sure you prioritize your horse's manners based on what they need to know right now, then add the upgrades as you continue to trust each other and grow. You are responsible for deciding your horse's education program, so make sure you select steps that make sense for the here and now first.

Additionally, it's a really good idea to take this type of training one step at a time, and try to start with initial contact first. I've known many horses who are equally difficult to catch in their stall or in a field, or have snapped and danced while being tacked up, yet were professional babysitters once their rider was aboard. Clearly many steps were skipped in their training process. While this is one possible shortcut when preparing a horse for the show pen, it isn't ideal for all of the people who may interact with your horse.

This brings us to our next point How does your horse act for other people? It's one thing if they maintain their good behavior when you're around them, but what about when other people interact with your horse? Let's take a look at how things may change when someone else is holding the reins.

Chapter 3: When Others Handle Your Horse

You may be thinking that you can skip this step completely because no one but you handles your horse. As long as you know how to adapt and work with their quirks, things will be fine, right?

For the most part, this is true. You might be willing to compromise on some of the finer points of politeness for the sake of focusing on more pressing issues. As I've noted, you need to be able to prioritize what you intend to teach your horse before you start the educational process. Just like the Billboard Hot 100, this list of priorities will continue to fluctuate and change. The goal is to not introduce too much at once in order to allow your horse to focus on one major skill at a time. And while this means we may have to calm that inner perfectionist who is looking to solve all of the problems immediately, it gives your horse a fair chance to learn everything well so that they fully understand each concept and can apply this new logic on their own.

It's a great idea to make sure your horse is willing to at least have a new human:

> Hold onto their lead rope without having an emotional meltdown
> Lead them around, regardless of how unfamiliar the area
> Touch their body, face, and feet
> Move around them, including moving equipment, talking, etc

When I've mentioned this in the past, other horse folks largely agree with me. However, I occasionally hear this line: *No one but me ever handles my horse, so why does it matter?*

First and foremost, your veterinarian and farrier would deeply appreciate it if they could examine and work with your horse without fearing for their lives. I realize some people do a majority of their diagnostics, treatment, and hoof trimming on their own, and I certainly don't object to that. But what about that one time when your horse does something truly magical and mysterious to themselves in the field and needs x-rays or stitches? What if you discover your horse needs shoes? What if you become injured and can't take care of your horse's hooves on your own?

These are a lot of "what ifs," and in a perfect world, they'll never happen. But my experience has led me to believe that needing a professional at some point is more or less inevitable. No matter how much you try to contain our horse and their bad manners to your own bubble, you will very likely need to have another person touch your horse at some point in their lives.

In fact, that other person might be a future caretaker of your horse. As much as we want to think that our fuzzy friends will live with us forever and ever, there may come a time when it makes sense for them to live with someone else, either in a lease situation or permanently. Generally speaking, it is easier to find a home for a horse who will allow other human beings to handle them than a horse who is allegedly trained, but won't come out of their stall for anyone but you.

Some horses seem to genuinely not care about who is handling them, as long as they aren't being hassled by this new person. Many horses in lesson stables, boarding barns, and training facilities see a rotating cast of characters each day, including stall cleaners, feeders, trainers, riders, vets, farriers, and other horse owners. As long as someone approaches them calmly and quietly, they're pretty accepting of some basic cues.

Other horses have been traumatized somewhere along the line. Belle is not a huge fan of men who are taller than her head, but our vet has been very patiently and kindly working with her to help her accept that he's one of the good guys. I don't know how or what happened, but this is something important to note if she ever leaves my care.

When your horse is uncomfortable with another individual handling them, they may refuse to stand still, and prance in place with their head up. They may try to bite or strike out with their feet to remove the perceived danger from their presence. They may absolutely refuse to move their feet, instead choosing to rear to dodge the cue to walk forward. Horses can conjure up some pretty effective evasion tactics for 1,000-pound creatures, and a lot of these reactions can be very dangerous for the horse and everyone and everything around them.

If your horse refuses to act reasonable when other individuals attempt to exist in their presence or ask them to do simple things like pick up a foot or accept a pat on the neck, it may be time for your horse to attend charm school– like the debutantes of yesteryear– to learn some manners.

It's not easy to find someone who is willing to play the role of guinea pig in your horse-handling experiments because horses can be scary. You need another person who is at least as skilled as you are in handling horses, who knows about timing and can deliver a cue to prevent absolute chaos. At the same time, it's important for your horse to just roll with it when someone asks them to lead forward the "wrong" way, or makes a simple perceived "mistake" in their routine.

Even if you don't distinctly foresee your horse needing to behave for another person, it's a great idea to prepare your beast for the potential of having to behave regardless of who is handling them. As my trainer has told me numerous times, "don't train a horse for yourself." This means that, when working with a horse to develop good manners and behaviors, it's important to have a horse that knows how to react to *what* you're asking, not the specific way you, personally, ask for it.

If you train a horse to only be handled or ridden by yourself, you are not doing that horse any favors in life. Imagine a toddler who only responds to being told "no" by a certain individual. And one day, that toddler is standing by an open gate by a busy road, alone, and they're scared. I'll end the scenario there because I honestly don't want to imagine it, but the point stands.

It may not be your main goal today or tomorrow, but if you're not sure how your horse will act when being handled by others, you might want to bump that experiment up on your priority list until you know for sure.

While you're at it, you might want to look further into how your horse acts and reacts when anyone or anything unfamiliar suddenly appears on their turf.

Chapter 4: General Interaction with People, Animals, and Strange Objects

You may be wondering when your horse is going to encounter other people and animals, and why you should worry. You may also be curious about what constitutes a "strange" object.

For some horses, people are strange objects. People come in different shapes, sizes, personalities, and noise levels. As humans, we acknowledge that each individual of our species is unique. We recognize tall, short, wide, thin, old, and young people as human beings. We recognize people in wheelchairs or strollers, we understand how mobility aids work, and we know that people come in different colors and wear different types of clothing.

Horses also come in different shapes, sizes, personalities, and noise levels. As humans, we will freely admit when a horse intimidates us. You may prefer to work with ponies only. Measuring less than 14.2 hands (or 58 inches) from hoof to withers, ponies are physically smaller than horses, yet often have double the orneriness. Some folks enjoy that. Others prefer working with gentle giant draft horses only. Just like humans, horses come in all sorts of packages, and sometimes, we feel more comfortable handling a specific type of package.

So let's flip that. If we have concerns about the type of horse we work with, why shouldn't horses be equally concerned about the humans they work with? In each case, the preferences aren't dictated by a weird bias or prejudice, but an understanding of the situation and what could go wrong. A human looks at an 18 hand (72 inches) horse standing with their head raised, nostrils flared, and eye whites showing, and makes a decision about whether they can safely handle this horse, given their experience. A horse looks at a child red-faced and crying in the aisleway, and makes a decision about whether they can safely interact with this being, given their experience. (Just a reminder–the Resources section will include links to general horse information, in case some of these terms are new to you!)

A horse's instincts tell it to assume that anything unfamiliar is very likely dangerous. Therefore, when your horse meets a baby, sees a human in a wheelchair, or hears the weird rustly sound of snow pants for the first time, they may be very concerned. In most cases, however, horses have a pretty good memory for knowing what is human, once they've been properly introduced.

The typical response for a horse who is encountering a new human-related situation is caution. They might refuse to get too close to the new person, instead stretching their long necks to sniff and explore the situation with their lips from what they feel is a safe distance. They might also snort, shake their head, and dance around a bit while they decide if walking up to this new being is a good idea. Most horses can be convinced to drop their apprehension with a few favorite treats, some kind words, and a few minutes to take everything in and process it. Allow them to approach on their own time while using their sense and instincts to suss things out, and many horses will acquiesce to meeting all sorts of new acquaintances–human and non-human.

On the other hand, there are horses who are far more intimidated by new friends. The most common reaction I've seen among horses who are being introduced to new humans is moving backward suddenly or bolting away from the potential danger. I've seen this type of behavior most often when introducing strollers or other types of child-toting equipment. A person in a wheelchair often looks like a person sitting down, which many horses recognize. They rarely react with interest until the chair actually starts rolling. A child in a stroller, however, comes with all sorts of different smells, sounds and motions, many of which are completely new to the average horse.

Again, you may be wondering why you need to figure out how well your horse deals with strollers or canes or snow pants. (That's a real thing, by the way– I once knew a horse who couldn't handle the swishy sound made by snow pants, track pants, or the down jacket I used to wear when doing chores in the winter months.)

Your horse may not have to deal with anyone else right now, but consider the following possible–and not so far-fetched–scenarios:
- Your horse needs to travel to see a new vet, farrier, or trainer
- You decide to move your horse to a barn where other people board their horses
- Your friend moves their horse into your private facility
- You add to your family, such as introducing a new child, spouse or partner
- You have an accident and need to use crutches or a cane for a bit
- Family comes to visit you
- You join a trail riding group that meets up regularly
- You start attending horse shows or 4H/Pony Club events
- You choose to lease your horse to an individual temporarily

- You sell your horse
- You pass away before your horse

I know some of those are pretty grim, and it's not my intention to bring us all down. However, each of these is a scenario I have seen play out in real life. Having a horse that can not only be handled by other people, as we discussed in the last chapter, but who can handle having other people around is beneficial in all of these situations.

The same goes for introducing your horse to other animals. I cannot think of a barn where I have worked or boarded where dogs and cats were not among the menagerie of creatures on premises. And yet, plenty of horses are terrified of each.

This makes perfect sense, really. Dogs and cats are predators, and behave as such. Horses are prey animals, and they are genetically pre-programed to believe never the twain shall meet. In many situations, the dogs and cats are more terrified of the horses than the horses are of the smaller creatures. Still, today's horses descended from terrier-sized creatures known as *eohippus*, so a strong sense of caution is very much present whenever horses encounter other barn creatures.

Again, the appropriate reaction is to sniff, snort, back up a little, and take a few moments for each creature to assess the other. Dogs may bark, circle, or play-bow as they work on this big, smelly puzzle. Cats frequently hiss or swat. Some cats have the sense to avoid horses entirely. Other cats will sleep in horse stalls, once they know who their friends are.

Some horses are more "fight" than "flight," and will aggressively attempt to seek out and destroy any smaller critter. I know more than one horse who will stop whatever they're doing to chase a cat. In only one case was this a friendly situation. I once worked with a young former race-horse who was obsessed with cats. Furthermore, the cats were obsessed with him. I found that I had to put the barn cats in the tack room when I was working with this horse because the minute one of his kitty friends entered the arena, he would run over to the cat and let it rub all over his face. Then they'd groom each other, which was just as awkward and difficult as you might expect it to be. Yet they insisted.

While you may not have to worry about dogs or cats in your barn at this particular moment, be aware that they will likely be present at other facilities and showgrounds. Cats in particular are helpful around barns and stable facilities as they help control the population of wild animals who stop by to check out the food and shelter situation. Then again, I know many horses who attack all types of uninvited guests, including rats and raccoons.

Your horse doesn't have to graciously accept all attention from other animals, but it is helpful if they approach them just as they do people– with curiosity and interest. Many horses are generally relaxed about meeting new animals, but the bleat of a goat, the sudden fan of a peacock's tail, or the array of noises made by a donkey may be a cause for concern. Having good manners will enable your horse to make good choices and react safely if they ever have the occasion to meet new friends.

Then there's the multitude of weird stuff that horses can potentially encounter in their world. It is impossible to shield horses from weird stuff because it is impossible to predict what a horse will consider "weird." Red, for example, has no problem with a lot of the things I personally find a bit unnerving. Those who have read my other books are familiar with his general unflappability, and how fascinating I think it is when he reacts to something. He's had umbrellas open in his face, balloons land on his head, plastic bags get stuck on his feet. He's stood stock still while teenage boys wrestled under his feet, he's snuggled babies, and he has no problem with wheelchairs, strollers, or those motorized toy cars that kids like to argue over more than actually drive. He's a friend to all he meets. You can put his blanket on upside down, inside out, and backwards if you feel like it.

Red is also very concerned with a particular set of work lamps that we keep in the arena during the winter months for those who don't need the full arena lighting. The arena measures 60 feet by 120 feet, so flicking on all of those lights is expensive. The smaller work lights provide plenty of light so folks can walk through the arena to the fields or other parts of the barn. Unfortunately, Red has decided they are evil and must be destroyed. He has pulled them out of their fixtures and destroyed the plugs several times. As I write this book, I'm currently working with him to convince him that these actions are not necessary. Just leave them alone. Progress is slow so far, but he's also very bored at present after having some time off due to frigid weather, so it's not a cut and dry training situation.

Nor will it ever be. Whenever you work to desensitize your horse to any specific item, person, or animal, something will go sideways. The garbage truck will pull up loudly. A bicycle will whizz by. The neighbor's dog will start barking. The wind will start blowing, or the temperature might change. This is why we continuously work with our horses to help them maintain equine good citizenship. Something about the situation will always be different, and your horse will have a choice of how to respond. Whether or not your horse registers this situation as dangerous or not, the goal is for them to respond in a way that is not dangerous in itself.

It's ok for your horse to get a little excited about new things. Even the most seasoned show horses tend to get a little perky when they unload from the trailer in a new place. Horses rely on their senses to stay alive, which means they have a lot to take in and process at once. You might feel overwhelmed when you show up at a new place, too. Who do these new faces belong to? What are others like here? New sounds and smells, accompanied by things you've never seen before are bound to be overwhelming, regardless of your species!

On the other hand, it is not ok for your horse to act in a way that is dangerous to you and everyone and everything around you. Your definition of "dangerous" might be a bit different at various points of your life, too. For example, I've known several trainers who greatly dialed back on the shenanigans they were willing to tolerate during their pregnancies.

The best way to ensure that your horse has praise worthy manners and can handle themselves in a variety of situations is to work with them as much as possible on their manners. This includes desensitizing them to different people, animals, objects, and places.

This doesn't necessarily have to be a Great Big Training Extravaganza, either. In many cases, I've had the opportunity to introduce a horse to a new person or thing just because it's there. One time, a barn owner had gotten a new tarp, and she was airing it over the fenceline. I immediately took Red over there so he could meet the tarp. A new hose, wheelbarrow, or even a differently-shaped feed bucket can become a fascinating learning experience, depending on what your horse has decided is threatening.

The goal is to always come into a situation expecting the best but anticipating the worst. That means knowing the possible reactions your horse might have while remaining calm and confident that this will be a non-issue. There's an old saying that horses can "smell fear," but I'm not sure that it's so much an odor or pheromone that they recognize, as much as the frozen, big eyed, non-committal, shaky way we often approach things when we're not sure what's going to happen next. Is the big horse going to walk past the scary plastic bag, or are we all going to get stitches tonight? There's no guarantee, and that can be intimidating for both horse and human.

When someone has more horse issues than they have solutions, we say they're "overhorsed." If you are overhorsed, it's a great idea to invoke the expertise of a professional. Whether you have a trainer come to you, drop your horse off at the trainer, or video chat with a trainer, you are still taking a very important step in helping your horse become an equine good citizen.

But here's the hard part. As I've mentioned several times, you'll need to do several challenging things simultaneously:
- Pay attention to your horse's bad behavior
- Determine if it's caused by something other than naughtiness

- Prioritize how essential it is to deal with this behavior
- Attempt to not obsess over the potential for disaster
- Keep your cool and move to a remote location
- Consider the most important situations to address with your horse
- Adjust as needed because your horse will probably also get an abscess or throw a shoe, or some other aspect of your life will need your attention for a week or so

It's going to be a process. Unless you are a professional, or can afford a professional to work with your horse every single day until all of their issues are sorted, it's going to be a long, arduous, ridiculous, frustrating process. You'll take one step forward, ten steps back, and show up on an entirely different path two days later.

But if we're being honest here, isn't that how our learning process goes, too? Did you learn how fractions work overnight? Probably not, but eventually, you got the concept of what "half" of something is, as well as the symbol: "1/2". It took a while for the words and symbols and ideas to have meaning, but once they did, you likely became a professional at precisely splitting any delicious food item in the school cafeteria.

Learning is rarely linear, which is why I mention that list of priorities changing frequently. This is understandably intimidating. But your goal is not to find perfection in training your horse, but to find moments in which you and your horse sync up and understand each other perfectly. With practice, these moments will get longer and longer. You and your horse will always have a miscommunication here or an attitude-driven disagreement there, because you are both living beings. But working on politeness, understanding, and good manners from the ground up can help you remain safe and regain clear communication quickly.

Now that you have a few things to look for and think about, let's start considering the next steps for helping your horse understand good manners. First, you'll need to really pay attention to your horse, along with your own actions and reactions, so that you can address the situation accurately and appropriately, or more specifically, without things escalating.

It's time to observe and analyze the bad-mannered horse, as well as the well-intentioned human who hopes to turn that naughtiness around.

SECTION 2: WHAT BEHAVIORS ARE YOU OBSERVING?

I've had this conversation many times:

Person: My horse is a jerk.

Me: Oh really? What are they doing?

Person: They're just nasty.

Me: Like biting you?

Person: No, just like being mean.

Me: When?

Person: I don't know, like all the time.

Me: What are you doing when they do this?

Person: Nothing! I'm just standing there!

Every single time, I give them a moment, then ask a very important question:

So, what am I supposed to do?

I don't say it to be a smart aleck, though I do usually ask with a sense of humor and empathy. But the question stands. You've just shared with me that your horse is a mean, nasty jerk when you are standing some-where in their presence.

We can only change a situation once we've recognized our current situation and decided what needs to be changed. I don't know how to tell a horse not to be a jerk. I know how to correct a horse who is biting, train a horse to stand tied patiently, and teach a horse that their winter blanket is not going to eat them, but I don't know how to convince a horse not to be mean. This is extra true when I have no context about when or how the horse is being "nasty."

I don't expect new horse people to use advanced veterinary terminology when describing whatever their horse is doing. But in order to train a horse, any professional needs to know what the horse is doing, what you would prefer it do instead, and how you're currently responding to the naughtiness.

There are many other factors to take into account when attempting to describe, diagnose, understand, and correct bad behavior, most of which I hinted at in the last section. Whenever you're experiencing equine naughtiness, it's important to also consider:

- Your horse's recent health changes
- Your recent health changes
- Weather changes
- Stabling changes
- Routine changes
- Feed changes
- Turnout changes

- The horse's background/training/experience
- Your background/training/experience
- The horse's past trauma
- Your past trauma
- What you're currently working on in other areas
- What's going on around you
- Where you're working
- How important changing this behavior is to you
- How stressed your horse is about this behavior
- How stressed you are about this behavior

Generally speaking, none of this is in your control. Most changes that are within our control occur not because we're feeling bored and want to change things up, but because a series of circumstances have conspired against us. It's usually not possible for us to help our horses understand why these things should make sense to them.

Then again, very little of what might cause a horse to engage their instincts and behave against their training makes sense. Therefore, we need to take a closer look at those things that we can control, such as identifying the behavior, reacting, and trying to stop it.

Let's dig in a little more to these areas to help suss out the full picture of your horse's misbehavior.

Chapter 1: What Does Your Horse Do That You Don't Like?

This is the easiest question of them all, but it's not as simple as it may appear. Horses are more creative than we give them credit for. While it would be great if our issues were cut-and-dry, like "My horse bites anyone who is wearing a blue hat," it's usually more, "My farrier wore a blue hat the other day, and my horse bit him, so then my farrier yelled at my horse, and the horse got all startled and started dancing in the aisleway but then slipped on the aisle footing and snapped the cross ties, and then my farrier's cart knocked over, so my horse bolted and ran across the arena while there was a lesson going on, and now I haven't been able to coax them out of their stall in three days. Also, my trainer has a price on my head because my horse knocked a little girl off her pony and her mother pulled her out of the lesson program."

If you're wondering if that really happened, the answer is yes, and I still feel terrible about it. The point is, however, that horses frequently misbehave in situational ways, rather than by doing one naughty thing. Even if the behavior seems straightforward– "my horse kicks his stall walls when another horse is led past his stall," there's likely a little more to it than that.

It's helpful for everyone involved if you carefully observe your horse's behavior from beginning to end. For example, if they seem to lose their sense of reason every time they walk down the aisleway of your barn, consider the scene and any potential triggers. What objects are present? Is the sun shining off of anything strange? Does the horse get weird when it passes a particular spot or stall? Are there other horses present? Are there other people or animals present? Does it happen any time of day, or only at certain hours? There are so many strange and unusual factors that can inspire behavioral issues in horses that it's a good idea to really pay attention not only to the priority issue of your horse freaking out, but to the full scene and action of the event.

The human brain tends to have a hard time processing a potentially traumatic event, like a large horse violently spooking in an aisleway, while remembering all of the details in minutiae, so don't feel bad if you can't remember whether Jennifer was standing by Patch's stall, or Hillary was pushing the wheelbarrow past Henry in the cross ties. But knowing that there were two people, one wheely, a squeaky object, and another horse involved can help you narrow down the options of what is offending your horse.

To illustrate, let's revisit the concept of a horse who kicks their stall wall when other horses are being led past. So far, so good. You're able to determine a definite stimulus for your horse's behavior. But try asking yourself more questions about the scenario. Does your horse kick every time a horse is led past? If the answer is yes, then congratulations! You've got a very clear situation!

In many cases, however, there's far more to it. Observation is key to helping unlock the secrets of why your horse is being so naughty. Consider the full situation, rather than the individual behaviors. It may be that your horse kicks when other horses are being led past their stall, but only when horses are being led past their stall in the morning as they're being turned out for a few hours. Then, when those horses are brought back inside, your horse paces and stall walks. And perhaps your horse was previously turned out in the morning, but for any number of reasons, they're now part of the afternoon turnout herd.

Your horse is reacting to the fact that they're expecting to follow a routine, but that routine has been disturbed. That doesn't mean that the kicking behavior is appropriate, but it now tells you what problem you're trying to solve, rather than wishing it was possible to temporarily glue a horse's feet to the floor.

When it comes to deciding what behavior you want to modify, you first have to figure out what that behavior is. In this example, we want to stop the kicking, but most importantly, we want to stop the horse from explosively sharing their feedback regarding the turnout schedule changes. If your horse is that unhappy about something, they'll find new ways to be reactive, even if you stop the initial behavior. Gluing your horse's hooves to the floor would– hypothetically– stop the kicking, but there's a good chance your horse would then find a new way to express their displeasure.

This is equally true of situations where the behavior is more explosive and sudden. I once knew–and most long-time equestrians have once known–a horse who was just fine until she wasn't. I was once commissioned to hold this type of horse for the farrier. Her owner was out of town, and as the tallest, youngest, and strongest person in the barn, I was given the honor. Things started out just fine. The horse was never exactly relaxed, but she stood still with me at the end of the lead rope. The first hoof was rebalanced, reshod, and reshaped with no problem. Then, as the farrier was rasping the second hoof, something changed. She started to get dancy and distracted. Every sound would be a reason for concern. Her

46

eyes became wider and wider, and her nostrils flared as her breath grew more rapid. It was at this point that she departed reality, heading straight up into the air on her hind legs.

This was, sadly, typical behavior for her any time she was asked to stand still for long periods of time. Farriers have a very delicate job of getting angles and pressure just right for a horse's anatomy and stride, so they tend to make many small adjustments to ensure the best performance and most comfort for each individual horse. Standing still for that long simply wasn't in this horse's wheelhouse.

The worst part was that for days after having her feet done, she would prance, kick, and nip at anyone who tried to touch her feet because she associated picking up her feet with the "torture" of standing still. Horses typically have the farrier reshape and rebalance their hooves every 6-8 weeks, so it felt like she was just becoming herself again when it would be time for another round.

There were three possible solutions here:

1. Tranquilize her every time someone needed to touch her feet
2. Throw a chain around her lip and have two people wrestle her down every time she tried to go up
3. Make sure she was adequately fed and exercised as much as possible prior to the farrier arriving, combined with taking multiple breaks to help her reset her head

Each plan has merit and challenges, so let's discuss in more detail:

Plan 1: On one hand, tranquilizing her means she'd be calm and sedate through the entire process. For the most part, sedation is a standard veterinary process with minimal risks.

On the other hand, many types of sedation require a veterinarian to be on premises. Furthermore, having her sedated each time her feet are cleaned– on a daily basis– means she would be eternally out of it.

Plan 2: Twitches and lip chains are often considered cruel, due to the way they pinch the horse's large top lip and twist around, tightening around the flesh. There are many wrong ways to do this, but if done right, a lip chain can actually calm a horse by releasing endorphins. The idea is to twist to the point where the horse is naturally non-resistant, then release so they can get lost in the sauce for a few.

However, many people take this approach with aggression and try to fight a resisting horse blow-by-blow. No matter how superhumanly strong your anger, adrenaline, and emotions make you in the heat of the moment, reflect back to the horsepower example I gave in the introduction. Your horse will either win this fight, or be prepared to die trying.

Plan 3: This is the most humane plan, obviously. It takes into consideration the real situation behind the behaviors–the horse is likely bored out of her mind standing in one spot for so long, so she's looking for interesting things to do. Then, once she's at the end of her mental and emotional tether, she acts out.

The problem with this method is that it could potentially take all day. And while I constantly preach the whole "it will take as long as it takes" rhetoric, your farrier does not care about training your horse. Your farrier wants to get through the day without being stepped on, to be paid fairly for each horse, and to go home to lie on their heating pad or ice pack for 2-3 hours. If you want your farrier to stick around all day while you take as many breaks as necessary to wind your horse down to have their feet touched, you'd best plan on paying them accordingly.

Ultimately, we ended up doing a little bit of all three at first. The horse was first lunged until she was content and relaxed. Then she ate her breakfast with a vet-approved dose of acepromazine in it. Once she seemed a little more chilled out than usual, two people would accompany her to the farrier—one to hold the lead rope, and the other to administer a lip chain as needed. When the horse started getting fussy during the visit, she was given a break to walk up and down the aisle. When she reared up, she was backed rapidly into the arena while her regular handler (taller and more experienced than I) would administer discipline. For this horse, that included sharp, tight jerks on the leadrope until she brought "all four to the floor" and relaxed through her neck.

But what about letting the lesson students touch her feet? It turns out, once the horse was no longer thoroughly traumatized by the process of standing still, she wasn't triggered as much by people touching her feet. Other than making sure only experienced riders handled her immediately following a farrier visit, we didn't need to tip-toe around her anymore, pun intended.

This was not accomplished in one visit, of course. All told, I'd say it was about a full year of following this type of program before everyone–the horse, the farrier, and the two handlers–felt comfortable with this routine. And though the horse has long passed through my life to another barn, I would not be surprised if the routine remains in place.

I tell this story to illustrate my meaning when I ask what your horse is doing that you don't like. You could say "rearing for the farrier," but that wasn't the issue here, was it? The real issue was a horse who was disinclined to stand still for long periods of time.

Furthermore, the answer wasn't "fix it." Instead, we did our best to make the horse comfortable with the process, so that everyone involved could remain safe. You can't force an animal the size of a horse to do something perfectly every single time. In fact, one might even argue that you can't force any animal to do something perfectly every single time. Can you make it through a pedicure silently, without shifting in your seat or letting your attention wander?

Instead, we helped the horse deal with the situation in the safest way possible. Do I love the fact that this plan included sedatives and lip chains? Yes and no. On one hand, my inner idealist wishes the horse could have been coaxed to accept and understand. On the other hand, regular farrier work and safety are equally necessary. The goal was to accomplish both without traumatizing the horse, and I think we achieved that.

I've gone a little bit past the starting point here with this example, but I wanted to explain how important recognizing the true nature of a horse's "bad" behavior can be. In some cases, yes, a quick tug on a lead rope or tap on the shoulder with a riding crop will be enough to return the horse to their thinking brain. In others, though, you may find yourself doing a lot of observational research, and trying out a lot of different angles in order to approach and address the true behavior with empathy and kindness.

Chapter 2: How Are You Reacting?

This question is a true test of one's humility because honesty is required. Quite frequently, when a horse starts misbehaving and acting out of instinct instead of intelligence, we humans follow suit. When the large, unpredictable beast starts acting as big and dangerous as we know it is, we stop thinking about analyzing and resolving situational behavior, and we do whatever it takes to save ourselves.

This may include doing things we've been told never to do, such as:
- Letting go of the lead rope or lunge line
- Running
- Curling into the fetal position with our arms over our heads
- Screaming

These are all things we're taught not to do during our first interaction with a horse, and yet it is our instinct to do all of them, simultaneously, when things get scary.

I would like to take this moment to humble myself by publicly admitting that I have done all of these. In fact, I have done some of them on purpose. Let's take them one by one to examine the merits and challenges.

Letting Go: The ramifications of this one are pretty obvious. When you let go of a horse, you no longer have any control over them. They will go where their currently overwhelmed brains take them.

However, if you are currently attached to a horse by a six foot cotton/poly blend rope, and that horse is getting ready to move at great speed, you should definitely let go, or risk being pulled by the horse. If you are currently in a cart or sleigh, that might be fun or festive, but when you're standing in a busy barn aisleway, it is significantly less jolly.

Running: Horses are prey animals, so something running towards them is often interpreted as a potential predator. They may kick or nip to rid themselves of the attacker. If something is running away from them, they frequently wonder why the herd is going that direction and try to join.

But if you are in an area in which a horse is going ballistic, and you are not directly involved in mitigating the situation, get out. Rapidly. Even at a run if you must. This is not one of those instances where we form a protective crowd around the panicked animal because that will intensify the situation.

Protective Positioning: Riding horses has helped me appreciate how much humans love the fetal position. Whenever we get overwhelmed, our bodies react by curling our skeletons around our vital organs. Even sitting astride a horse, the human body has a tendency to curl up when it feels unstable. The act of riding involves the relaxation and control of every muscle group, though, so this position is impractical for riding purposes.

On the ground, however, it's absolutely ok to get small to avoid a tantru-ming horse. If you're not in a position to handle the situation, get as far out of it as possible and protect yourself. That might mean crouching in the corner of a wash rack, or trying to make yourself invisible in a trailer. Protect yourself, always. If you need to wear a helmet, gloves, and a protective body vest while handling your horse when they're working through bad behavior, by all means, do!

Screaming: Horses do not care for loud, sudden noises– again, due to their prey animal status. They are easily startled, and their reaction to loud, sudden noises might be exactly what you're trying to work on, behaviorally speaking.

Sometimes, however, we can take advantage of a horse being easily startled by loud, sudden noises in order to distract them from whatever other terrible behavior they're demonstrating. Just like humans, horses can be trained to recognize "cease and desist" noises, such as roaring "QUIT!" or "NO!" or "BAD!" in a loud, assertive tone. One of my trainer friends calls it her "Horse Mom Voice," while another calls it his "Yes, Sir Voice." I'm not saying it's wise to horror-film holler, but loud voice commands can be used effectively to stop a horse from getting too deep into their instincts and emotions.

You've also likely heard that horses and other animals can "smell fear" or "sense nervousness." There is some truth to that. Horses communicate through body language, so they're frequently scanning our own actions to get a feel for how they should react. If there's a loud, sudden noise and you jump nervously, chances are high that your horse is going to also react. However, if there's a loud, sudden noise, and you have absolutely no reaction whatsoever, your horse is more likely to assume that everything is perfectly fine.

Horses are also not big fans of physical punishment. Yes, absolutely, there are times when a well-placed chain or whip can deliver an important and humane message, but that message should ultimately be, "pull your brain together, Fluffy, and work with me here!" If you approach a horse with these tools from a standpoint of punishment for their behaviors, they may not be as understanding.

We'll get more into conditioning and "reward versus punishment" shortly, but for now, remember that horses are instinct-based creatures. When something unpleasant happens to them, their ultimate goal is to get out of that situation. Approaching bad behavior with anger and resentment is far more likely to escalate the dangerous actions of both human and beast.

When your horse starts doing whatever it is that you want them to stop doing, pay close attention to what you're doing as a reaction. Is it possible that what you're doing isn't effective at all, or potentially counter-effective? If your horse pulls backwards on the lead rope, and the first thing you do is let go time after time, you'll eventually teach your horse a nifty way to get away from you, and your horse will have taught you a new way to fear them.

It may also be that what you're doing is escalating things. This may not be through intentional punishment, but the way you react may actually cause the horse to become more agitated or afraid. Horses look to their herd leaders for cues on how to act when things aren't right, and if you're lying on the floor crying, your horse may assume things are really, really bad.

And yet, looping back around to the beginning of this chapter, there are situations where letting go and lying on the floor might not just be your instinct, but your best choice. This is why horse training is so complicated.

Much like Kenny Rogers in *The Gambler*, you, "gotta know when to hold 'em and know when to fold 'em." This takes a lot of practice and many mistakes, as any professional can attest. As I've said before and shall continue to say, if you are over-horsed, it is absolutely appropriate to call in a professional. Just make sure you're ready to be honest with them when they ask how you act when your horse is being naughty!

Chapter 3: What Have You Tried?

At first, this may seem like an identical question to "how are you reacting." After all, the way you react is what you've tried, right?

Without arguing over semantics, I'd like to emphasize on the word "tried." This is to indicate that you actually put thought and physical effort into correcting your horse's behavior, rather than letting your own instincts take over.

At the same time, if your instinct is to slap your horse in the face when it tries to bite you, that's important information for any and all parties involved in solving this riddle. And please note that I'm not judging you for this counterstrike in the least. For many of us, it's quite natural to swat at something approaching our personal space as a protective measure. In most cases, the spontaneous blow a human can administer to a horse in this situation is minimal compared to the damage the horse was about to impart. And, in quite a few cases, it's all that's needed to convince the horse to reconsider that particular behavior.

That's not to say I'm advocating for beating your horse in the face. In fact, I urge you not to beat your horse at all, ever. Instead, I'm saying that it is important to pay attention to both your reactions and actions, and the role they play in diminishing or escalating a horse's behavior.

Furthermore, I'd like to make a distinction between a bump or nudge and a slap or punch. The former is setting a type of physical boundary– "you may not enter this zone or continue this nonsense." The latter is actual abuse, likely stemming from an explosive combination of emotions including but not limited to: frustration, anger, regret, confusion, fear, blind rage, or that feeling you get when you don't know exactly the right thing to do at the right time. The velocity with which a bump and a slap are delivered also varies greatly, as does the location of delivery. Swatting your horse on the rump is exactly as effective as swatting a toddler on the rump– they may act as if this is the most sadistic injustice they have ever experienced, or they may completely ignore you.

However, the act of setting a physical boundary with a large body part is a significant communication strategy between horses. Nipping, swinging your hindquarters into an offending party's face, and pinning the ears back while flaring the nostrils and showing the whites of the eyes are all common ways horses tell each other, "Back off! I mean it! Right now!" Swatting, bumping, nudging, and pushing your horse are all similar to the equine response of "hey! Stop being a jerk!" The difference between communicating with your horse in equine body language and straight up beating your horse boils down to education, duration, and intent.

Let's look at these concepts in a little more detail:

- **Education**: By this, I mean how educated are you in this method of behavior modification? The difference between teaching and trauma lies in delivering your response in a balanced, calm, reinforcing manner, which in turn requires perfect timing. This can be daunting even to seasoned professionals. Mistakes will be made, and there are a lot of "right choice/right time" situations that have the potential to escalate into a disaster. In order to properly "reform" a horse's naughty behavior, it's important that you feel skilled and confident enough to conduct their training.

- **Duration**: Making physical contact with your horse in any manner should last seconds, not minutes. When we're riding, we'll kick or bump our horses with the heel of our foot to urge them to go forward. We do not raise our legs to hip height and repeatedly slam giant spurs into our horses' flanks unless the situation absolutely calls for it. If your "punishment" or "correction" method lasts more than a moment, it very well may be—however unintentionally—escalating the situation. The goal is not to make the horse regret their actions, but to understand that they made the wrong decision. You're here to help the horse choose wisely, not be left without a choice.

- **Intent**: Again, you must leave your emotions and ego behind when attempting to train horses. There will be many shiny, glowing moments of success that are quickly overshadowed by your horse doing *exactly* the thing you've been trying to talk to them about. There may be times when you find yourself question- ing all of your life decisions up to that exact moment. But you

57

can't let your horse know about it. In many cases, all they are aware of is that some collection of cells in their brain made their whole body do something all at once. And, if they're doing this behavior on purpose, it's likely because they've learned that doing this behavior is advantageous in some way. Again, this is why observing and understanding why this behavior is occurring is so important– if you know what your horse's intention is, you can act with equal intention. Beating your horse in a fit of rage will very likely stop that specific behavior, but it's not a long-term fix. It's the start of an entirely different set of problems. Reacting and acting consciously and purposefully when your horse misbehaves gives you the chance to stop that behavior and help your horse understand what better choices are available.

So, if you are asked by a trainer, barn owner, vet, or concerned party asking, "What have you tried?," the best response is the truth. Either it's working, it hasn't done anything, or it has made things significantly worse. In most cases, having the assistance of experts is the best way to alleviate situations where nothing seems to be working, or things have escalated.

Other things to mention under the umbrella of "what have you tried" include:
- Nothing
- Ignoring the horse when they are misbehaving
- Letting the horse "work it out on their own"
- Immediately returning your horse to their stall/pasture
- Requesting someone else deal with it
- Using any gadgets or gizmos recommended by your horse buddies
- Feeding the horse when they are misbehaving

None of these responses are inherently "wrong," though some horse professionals may wish to persuade you otherwise. I like to believe that we are all doing our best, and though we may make mistakes, it's important to educate ourselves and maintain forward motion and progress in our understanding. So, while someone might emphatically explain that, "doing xxx is the worst possible thing you could ever do for your horse, ever," I encourage you to take that with a grain of salt, unless you are admittedly beating your horse in a wanton rage.

By keeping track of all of your reactions and actions regarding your horse's misbehavior, you can better identify the severity and frequency of the problem, as well as note what doesn't work, what works a little bit, and what makes things worse. From there, you can choose a new course of action for both you and the horse to either work through or work around the problem.

Now that we have an acute awareness of the behavior, as well as accountability on our own part as the human involved in these mischievous moments, let's attempt to step inside the horse's mind to get their side of the story.

SECTION 3: WHAT IS YOUR HORSE TRYING TO TELL YOU?

From your point of view, what your horse is doing is scary, and you need them to cease and desist immediately. But what's going on from your horse's point of view?

Unfortunately, they can't really tell us what set them off in human words. However, watching your horse's facial expressions, body language, and overall movement can tell us more about what they're experiencing.

It may seem at this point that working with horses involves a lot of observing and understanding. This is correct. We are two parties who share no common language, attempting to communicate about activities that are unnatural to both of us.

Imagine you are in a foreign country for the first time. You recognize some of the words in their language, but certainly not enough to try to string together a sentence. Let's say you're enjoying your visit, strolling along a city street during a patch of drizzle, when a sudden gust of wind blows under your umbrella, carrying it off into a nearby sewer drain. Now what do you do? You certainly have the option to ignore the situation and carry on. You can buy a new umbrella. Or you can try to enlist the help of a resident by explaining your situation. How do you convince a stranger who speaks a different language that your umbrella is in the sewer? Even if you used the right words, they'd likely assume you were joking, mad, or mistaken. It's not a common enough scenario that you'd be able to adequately pantomime while using broken phrases in an unfamiliar language.

Let's rearrange this scenario slightly, and replace the human with a horse. And not only are they not sure why you're telling them there's an umbrella in the sewer, their very instincts are telling them that things flying around is a big problem and they need to get out of there right away. You're not going to be able to pantomime with your horse. You don't have the luxury of a phone translation app, either. What can help you in this situation is a general understanding of your horse's physical communication methods.

Not only does a horse's body language help us understand that they're upset in the first place, but frequently, they're attempting to communicate a very specific issue. Let's take a look at some of the ways horses try to explain things to us via facial expressions, overall body language, and the ways in which they might be moving their bodies.

Chapter 1: Facial Expressions

When we think of horses, we tend to think of them standing nobly, calmly, and blissfully. We don't often think of horses with eyes rolling, nostrils flared, jaws gaping, and ears pinned tightly against their heads.

Those types of scenes are reserved for heroic battle sculptures and stirring artwork, right?

As is frequently the case, art imitates life, and those dramatic warrior horse expressions do, in fact, exist. However, most horses are a bit more subtle in their day-to-day facial communications, which makes observing and understanding their behavior so interesting and important.

When we talk about a horse's facial expressions, this includes their ears, eyes, nostrils, and mouth. All of these parts of a horse are expected to move at some point in time, so this is not as dire as counting how many times your horse blinks, or every swivel of their ears. Instead, we're looking for remarkable expressions and their connection to different behaviors.

There are a few general guidelines about what a horse's ear position, amount of visible eye white, and nostril or mouth activity might mean. However, there are exceptions to every rule. For example, Appaloosa horses sport breed-specific physical characteristics that range from their spotted coat and thin manes, to naturally visible eye whites. An Appaloosa may appear shocked, judging from the appearance of their eyes, but they might actually be feeling 100% nonchalant. Some types of Arabian horses have larger than average nostrils; this trait serves well when performing in endurance-type sports, and has nothing to do with their overall attitude and sense of well-being.

As a result, it's a great idea to learn how to familiarize yourself with the overall message of a horse's body language. Of course, the best way to do that—in my experience—is to learn the various positions and expressions of each part of the face in order to put together and decode your horse's attempt to communicate with you.

A horse's ears have an impressive range of motion, and they can move independently. Typically a horse's ears swivel forward and backward in order to hear everything that is going on around them. While the position of a horse's eyes provides it with an expansive range of vision, the ears pivot like little satellite dishes to pick up any and all nearby transmissions. So, if your horse is standing still, looking otherwise calm but you notice their ears are twisting around a bit, this doesn't necessarily mean anything is immediately wrong but that your horse might need to be reminded that they need to pay attention to you, first. This can usually be accomplished with a little "QUIT" command, tap on the shoulder, light pop of the lead rope, or in Red's case, calmly saying, "My dude, hello" and waving. Whatever works for that particular horse.

If the ears swivel towards the rear, stay facing the rear, and start to lower closer and closer to the ground, your horse is likely expressing displeasure. Generally speaking, the flatness of the ears is directly indicative of how upset they are, but again, this can change from horse to horse. In many cases, ears that are turned backward but still upright are similar to a human glare or strong side-eye, while ears that are invisibly tucked against the horse's skull are what we might deem "about to go nuclear" in another human. Ears that are perked straight upwards may mean the horse is hyper-focused on a particular sound, which can be a problem if they decide the source of that sound is potentially dangerous.

Looking at a horse's eyes will also give you some indication of how relaxed or focused they are. A non-threatened horse will generally look around at their surroundings. They may or may not move their heads to get a closer look at something that's moving, or to follow their ears to determine what made a particular sound. For the most part, a horse looking around, observing their surroundings is a good thing. If your horse becomes hyperfocused on a single point of interest, raising their head to get a better look, you might need to remind them that they need to follow your lead, again with a light vocal or physical reminder to pay attention to you. On the other hand, if your horse's head shoots straight up, exposing their eye whites as their eyes bulge outward, that's a very common sign that they feel very threatened, and they're close to acting upon that threat.

Nostrils can be tricky, not only because of the difference in shape and size between different horses, but because some horses are what I call "naturally woofle-y." A "naturally woofle-y" horse is literally nosey– instead of checking out the smells that come to them, they're on the lookout for something untoward and their rapidly flapping nostrils make a soft "woof-woof-woof" sound. Horses have a keen sense of smell, and just as their ears work as radars, their noses are constantly scanning the scents that float by for signs of danger or deliciousness. Horses can detect both enemies and the presence of food through scent, so it's common for a horse to occasionally take in a few wide, deep breaths in order to analyze a smell. But, if your horse has their nostrils flared to maximum capacity, it's a very good sign that their fight, flight, or freeze instinct has engaged. They're not just reading the room at this point, but concentrating on a particular threat.

Mouth activity is usually more straightforward. If the horse is actively gnashing its teeth or trying to nip at something, that is nearly always a sign that they are experiencing discomfort or anger. I personally cannot recall a case in which a horse chomped its teeth continuously or in the direction of a particular stimulating object in glee, but I don't want to exclude any particularly expressive horses, so I won't say "always." You may find your horse chomps repeatedly when you're tightening the girth of your saddle. This could be a sign of discomfort, or just a bad habit your horse has picked up along the way. If the behavior is new, you might want to have them evaluated for ulcers, as this is a common way horses communicate belly pain.

A horse may stand quietly and chew with their mouth closed. This is frequently a sign of pleasure or being fully relaxed. Despite what some jokesters may try to tell you, horses are not ruminants, so they are not chewing their cud. They're simply moving their jaws because they're comfortable with what's going on around them. Happy horses may yawn or stick their tongue out, as well.

Then there are the many expressive faces horses pull when you've found their favorite scritchy-scratch spot. Horses can twitch their skin to rid themselves of bugs, they roll in dirt, sand, or mud for that deep, full-body itch relief, and they shake their entire body like dogs to flick debris from their body. They use their lips, teeth, and sometimes their hind legs to take care of tickly spots.

But there are some places they can't reach, and when you find those spots with your hands or curry comb, your horse will let you know by contorting their entire body to maximize the pleasure. They'll wiggle their lips from side to side, or smack them together while nodding their heads. They may put their upper lip straight up in the air, like they're smiling. Known as Flehemen Face, this expression actually increases their ability to smell, and can be associated with a very enjoyable grooming session, accidentally eating something they did not enjoy, or acknowledgment that a nearby mare is in estrus. My best advice in moments like these is to pull out your camera and take a few photos of your horse being goofy and happy because these are the moments you'll cherish forever.

In time, you may find yourself almost subconsciously tuned in to your horse's facial expressions. As a child, I was always fascinated by the seasoned horse people who could tell their horse to "knock it off" without looking up from grooming or tacking up. It is possible to become so tuned in to your horse's body language that you don't necessarily need to stop what you're doing to fully assess the complete message. Much as humans can learn other human languages with time, practice, and exposure, you may be able to learn not only your horse's method of communication, but vernacular and accent, as well.

That being said, learning new languages is easier for some individuals, and harder for others. You are not a bad horse person for not picking up what they're putting down. It can take years of daily interaction with horses to really get a feel for what they're telling us, and some horses are more stoic while others are drama queens in their communication styles. You may need a translator– in the form of a trusted friend, trainer, or vet– to help you really appreciate your horse's vocabulary.

I've included a selection of corresponding articles and videos in the Resources section to provide a visual example of some of the things I've mentioned here. This can help you understand your horse's facial expressions better, and over time, you'll likely appreciate your horse's personality, opinions, and triggers enough to appreciate even more subtle expressions and commentary.

Chapter 2: Body Language

Technically speaking, facial expressions are part of the overall concept of body language, but I wanted to address what a horse's face is doing and what their body is doing separately because there can often be a disparity between the two.

As prey animals, a horse's first reaction to warning signals going off in their brain is to stand stock still and analyze the situation, generally through their senses of hearing, sight, and smell. Hence the pricked ears, wide eyes, and flared nostrils. Unless you look at the horse's face, you may not be aware that they are paying attention to something besides you.

That being said, there are some subtle differences between a horse standing stock still because they have no desire to move otherwise, and a horse who is working out whether or not it's time to bolt. The main difference is usually the amount of tension in your horse's body. A relaxed horse might be standing with its neck in a comfortable, natural position. They might have a hind leg relaxed, standing with one toe cocked and resting their weight on their other three legs.

A horse who is working out the probability of danger will likely have their head raised with their neck tall and vertical. They'll stand very upright, shifting their weight to both rear legs so they can launch in the appropriate direction to get away from impending doom.

A horse's body positioning can also tell you if they're experiencing discomfort, physically or mentally. Horses are instinctually programmed to move away from pressure, which we'll discuss a bit more in the section about training methods. If your horse is swinging their front or hind end away from you, that may be their way of telling you that something's wrong, and it would be great if you could investigate the situation further.

The word "discomfort" can mean a lot of different things, though. For example, a horse who has a sore hoof due to an abscess or bruise may attempt to move the offending body part as far away from you as possible. They'll often shift their weight away from the sore side, or wave that leg in the air in an attempt to relieve the tremendous pressure and pain within their hoof. A horse who is back-sore, experiencing skin irritations like rubs or fungus, or having a stomach ulcer flare up, may scoot away from the pressure of the brush when you're grooming them. A horse who doesn't want their face or ears touched will do their best to remove them from your reach.

Your horse also has a singular communication device that we often forget: the tail. When we think about tail language, we typically think of a dog wagging their tail, or a cat puffing up their tail in alarm. Similarly, horses can be very expressive with their tails when the moment calls for it.

A horse's tail consists of the dock, which is part of the spine, and the skirt, which is the flesh and hair that comprise the exterior of a horse's tail. Tails can be very different from horse to horse, with some breeds having more vertebrae than others. Appaloosas tend to grow sparse, short tails, while Friesians and Gypsy Vanners have an unmerciful amount of tail (according to their groomers).

Muscles connecting along the horse's spine extend through the tail so that the horse can move it at will. Typically, a horse will swish their tail to ward off flies and other bothersome pests. They may use their tails as fans to circulate air around themselves on a sweltering day. Part protection and part air conditioning, a horse's swishing tail may mean nothing more than "it's a bit hot and buggy out here."

However, a tail can be used to communicate very exciting information. A horse who is angry will swish their tail aggressively. This differs from normal swishing due to the frequency and ferocity of the action. A horse who is extremely excited may raise their tail upwards and move rapidly with extended strides to demonstrate their pleasure, confusion, or fury.

Horses can also learn that humans find tail swishing threatening. I have known an experienced lesson horse or two who has tried to play the "I'm intimidating!" act when they simply want to continue hanging out in their stall or pasture.

Speaking of, when you enter your horse's stall, pasture, or enclosure, how do they respond? Do they turn their backsides to you and act like you aren't there? If you have cats at home, you may be familiar with this body positioning. It's a common expression of "I am displeased, and your presence is not alleviating this displeasure" in the animal kingdom. Horses generally exhibit this type of behavior when they're attempting to avoid leaving their current situation, frequently because they don't want to go to work. This may be due to pain or discomfort, or a bad habit they've picked up through their life experiences, so it's important to observe all of your horse's overall behavior to determine if this is normal for them, or a sign of possible trouble.

Now let's consider what happens when you interact or work with your horse. Does your horse pay attention to quite literally everything around themselves instead of you? When you mount up, does your horse scoot away from the mounting block quickly, or relax and let you get adjusted? A horse who is easily distracted can be dangerous, since they're clearly not paying attention to the person in charge (you). The entire purpose of training is to encourage a horse to trust and communicate with you, so when they're scanning their surroundings and come across something to react to, they're not in a position of trust or communication– they're preoccupied and absent-minded. It's more or less the equine equivalent of holding onto a lit fuse, but not knowing what it's connected to, hoping that the thing that goes pop at the end will be manageable.

Your horse may be exceptionally distracted in a new environment, or when new horses enter its presence. That's a temporary reaction to understandably over-stimulating situations. But if your horse is regularly mistaken for a yearling stud due to its behavior, prancing, dancing, and wildly googly-eyeing everything on a daily basis, it is time to take some important next steps in training.

Chapter 3: Movement

There is a fine line between body language and movement, but for the purpose of this discussion, body movement refers to specific gestures and actions a horse may perform when they're being obstinate, naughty, or particularly communicative.

Many horses give warning signals before they enter attack mode. For example, a horse who is thinking of kicking out with their hind legs, or bucking to bring their hindquarters fully in the air may hunch their rear end, pick up their hind legs rapidly, and even wag a raised leg in the air to mimic the action of a kick. Generally speaking, these actions are accompanied by backward ears to say, "Hey friend, I'm tolerating this, but not for much longer. Something needs to change."

A horse who is about to leave the premises in a hurry may prance in place or side to side as they figure out the best way to exit the situation. Horses may also wiggle side to side when they're trying to get away from an uncomfortable situation, such as a farrier asking them to pick up a sore leg, or a vet trying to administer a shot.

Backing quickly is another fun equine expression of disdain. And of course, by "fun," I mean "annoying and potentially dangerous." Horses are very capable of moving in reverse, barring certain spinal or lameness situations, and when they feel threatened, they can pull some *Smokey and the Bandit*-level maneuvers. While they can't move backward quite as quickly as they can forward, it's still fast and powerful enough to snap a breakaway halter or light cross ties, or cause serious damage to the muscles, tendons, and bones in your arms, shoulder, and back.

In most cases, the direction your horse wants to move will indicate the source of their terror or discomfort. As mentioned, horses move away from pressure, real or perceived. Sometimes, normally well-behaved horses can get a bit squiggly when they're trying to avoid something unpleasant. Ideally, your horse will give you plenty of clues about their emotions, especially when you combine their facial expressions, body language, and movement into a complete message.

By observing both the scene around you and your horse's attempts at communication, you can generally piece together what is triggering this response, and what's about to happen. This may take time, and while often it is obvious after the fact that Patch nipping at Henry, while Henry was spooking at Hillary pushing the wheelbarrow, caused Jennifer to scream, which in turn spooked Henry, which then caused your horse to rear and snap the cross ties, these multiple steps to doom may not lead to an immediate conclusion in the heat of the moment. As you watch your horse slide and stumble as it attempts to gain purchase to launch into a gallop on a concrete aisleway, you are not going to be thinking, "hmm… I wonder how this happened, and whether my horse provided obvious body language that I missed."

Instead, it's going to be a long process of watching and noticing subtle differences in your horse's behavior when they're relaxed, feeling good, uncomfortable, or in a rotten mood. Watching multiple body parts and movements simultaneously may feel complicated at first, but you'll likely start to recognize patterns pretty quickly. If your horse whips their head to the left to nip at you as you're tightening the girth every single time you tighten the girth, but no other time, the cause of the reaction is very clear.

On the other hand, a horse who doesn't want to do something may exhibit similar body language cues in order to explain a simple message of, "I don't want to; you can't make me." So how do you determine if your horse is triggered by a significant stimulus and needs to be desensitized to a situation, or if they're being ornery and need to be trained to give up the attitude?

That's where the rest of the body language package comes in. Your horse's facial expression can tell you a lot about how they're actually feeling. Are their teeth bared in anger or frustration, or are their eyes practically rolling in their heads because they've lost control of their physical reactions due to fear? Are they actively attempting to get away from something that has frightened them, or are they stoically refusing to do what is being asked?

A horse who is afraid will generally act on pure instinct, while a horse who is being stubborn will often act deliberately evasive– that is, until they are provoked into feeling threatened, at which point pure instinct will take over. For this reason, horse training can be challenging. Knowing that there's a grey area between thoughtful and instinctive reactions, and understanding exactly where and how generous or tiny your horse's grey area is, can be one of the most important things to grasp when working with an ill-behaved horse.

When we're confronted with our horse's bad behavior, we often feel pressured to do something about it right then. But that's not how horses work. Yes, it's important to take care of the current situation immediately, clean up any messes, and make amends as necessary. But the process of observing, understanding, and finding the right course of action for changing the offending behavior isn't going to happen overnight. Instead, it's going to be a process, and it might just take a village, as the saying goes.

SECTION 4: EVALUATING THE STAGES OF NAUGHTINESS

So far, I've referred to your horse's behavior in relation to your comfort level in somewhat vague terms. "If you think you can handle it," "you can call in a trainer," "if you don't feel comfortable," etc. Now we need to differentiate between the stages, levels, and potential escalation of your horse's behavior to determine where this behavior lies.

In order to do this, we need to have a full picture of what's happening, why it's happening, how your horse reacts, how you react, and how much warning you get before the naughtiness occurs. In each preceding section, we've discussed what to look for, how to look for it, and potential interpretations. This is how we determine how serious things are, and what our next steps may include. This is why I urged you not to sell your horse and move into a cave–this is the fun part!

You may be thinking that "fun" is the last word you'd use to describe your horse's behavior, and you might be concerned about my mental health for even associating "fun" with what is currently happening. Please note that I'm not making light of any dangerous situation– it's just that this is the point where you truly become a horse person, deciphering a strongly worded and heavily coded message from a four-legged fuzzy beast into behavior that makes sense and can be redirected. This is the moment the sleuth solves the case; the mystery is solved, and now everyone can proceed with the truth out in the open.

Therefore, we need to pull together all of our observations thus far:

Step 1: What behavioral problems does your horse have? How is your horse in their stall? Can you and other people handle your horse without fearing for your lives? Are you aware of any particular triggers or scenarios that set your horse off?

Step 2: What is your horse doing? Are they bolting, kicking, rearing, spooking, biting, becoming uncatchable, or freestyling their own particular brand of misbehavior?

Step 3: What are you doing and what have you already done? From your own instinctive reactions to actual attempts to provide redirection to your horse's behavior, reflect on what you do when your horse acts undesirably.

Step 4: What are your horse's "tells?" What are they doing right before disaster strikes?

Step 5: How urgently does this behavior need attention? How much time and effort are you able to invest into this situation?

The order of these steps is somewhat arbitrary, because there might be a lot of watching, observing, reflecting, changing your mind, and watching again to see if you observe something different, or if you had it right the first time. The human memory is an unreliable narrator, especially when our brains are super-charged on emotions or adrenaline.

You may wish to keep a journal or chart of things that you observe in order to figure out what the pattern is. As I've said many times, the situation may be bigger or more complex than you have imagined, and it won't change if you're not working with your horse on the thing that's setting them off.

I once worked with a lovely Thoroughbred ex-racehorse who was consistently lovely, curious, affectionate, and obedient. His natural posture was head up, ears pricked, woofle-ing around to find interesting smells, but he kept his feet and teeth to himself. One day, as I was cleaning his feet, his head shot up further than I could've imagined, he yanked his hoof away from me, charged backwards to the end of the cross ties, snapped the cross ties, turned himself around and bolted into our indoor arena, where he galloped himself in circles before stopping and walking over to me like nothing had happened.

I assumed–foolishly, of course–that he had been spooked by something I couldn't see when I was bent over, and we spent the rest of our work session sorting out hoof picking and cross ties so I could attempt to recreate the source of his panic. Other than being a little wary and snorty about ending up in the cross ties again, there was no encore performance.

I even further foolishly assumed that the issue was closed and done when it didn't happen again...at least, until it did happen again.

I will skip the long and arduous process of figuring it out because it took several months and experimentation to discover that the horse had allergies, and the combination of mucus drainage and almost invisible hives in the thick hair around his ears that were being irritated by the halter when he threw his head up, caused him to freak out. Horses regularly spook at the noise made when they break wind, so this is not entirely out of character for the species. It just wasn't the first thing anyone would have considered for a potential training issue.

The horse in question was brought back to physical health with a series of allergy shots and antibiotics to treat a mild sinus infection, and afterwards, retraining him to stand politely in the cross ties was a little bit of a process. Since we'd been looking in the wrong direction, he had worked up a bit of a trauma response to being tied. He expected serious pain and itchiness on his head and ears, and he expected that there would be yelling and consequences when he bolted because his fuzzy little brain and body couldn't handle the discomfort any longer. As a result, he was nervous in the cross ties for a long time. Still, we spoke to him kindly, reassured him, stayed calm around him, and let him sniff out the situation until he was satisfied it would be all right in the end.

Once you've figured out what's going on, you can gauge what the ideal next steps for you and your horse may be. Let's walk through the stages of naughtiness to get a feel for where you are now, and what you might need to do to enact change.

Chapter 1: Things You Can Improve Alone

Before we get started, I'd like to remind you that no horse person should feel that they have no choice but to "deal with it alone." There can be a million reasons why you might not consider it feasible to work with your horse's behavior problems on your own, including:

- Your age/the horse's age
- Your health/the horse's health
- Outlying conditions, like being pregnant, coming back from an injury/surgery, etc–again, considering both you and the horse
- Your experience with horses
- Your own sense of fear and danger

There's an old saying in the equine community: "Green plus green equals black and blue." The meaning behind this saying is that pairing an inexperienced horse with an inexperienced handler frequently results in injury. While I've mentioned several times throughout my books that bumps and bruises are borderline inevitable, we equestrians don't actively seek injury or threat to our personal health. The choices you make and boundaries you set may be based on the factors I've listed above or not– know that the choices you make are valid as long as they honor the safety and well-being of you, your horse, and any bystanders.

However, there are some instances wherein you might need to at least reinforce behaviors alone. For example, if your horse is a stall kicker, it is unreasonable to think that a trainer or behaviorist will come to your barn every time your horse starts beating on the walls. Instead, there may be times that you have to enact whatever communication and correction methods your professional has assigned to you.

That, however, is different from coming up with your own plan for resolution and acting on it. I've said that working with horses is often a curious thing, in that you may think you're going to work on this or accomplish that today, but your horse will alert you that you have another think coming. This is true under saddle, in hand, and when working on attitude issues.

A horse who doesn't want to do something–anything!- will often go out of their way to make sure they don't have to. So, once your horse has made up their mind that they are going to react to a certain scenario or trigger, they will avoid having to learn any other options. Just as you might take a stubborn toddler by the hand and walk them into the grocery store while they're having a meltdown, you might need to consistently keep your horse's attention focused and feet moving forward (or not moving at all, depending on the situation). That can be difficult.

Assess how comfortable you are leading your horse. How well do you think you can gain and hold your horse's attention? How comfortable do you feel with tools like stud chains and lunge whips? Do you have enough control of your emotions that you can repeat the same two steps forward and a hundred steps back for hours, days, or months?

Once I pulled Red from the field where he was slowly being starved and took him to my friend's barn, he decided he was "Home." As in, he would not leave the property. In many cases, once a horse is "Home," they quite rightly don't venture out. But I had plans to the contrary. I wanted to take him on trail rides at the local nature preserves, and I wanted to drive him over to a nearby barn that had a warm indoor arena in the winter. Additionally, it's a good idea to have a horse that's willing to hop on a trailer in case of a medical emergency!

But, Red wasn't having it. Each time I attempted to load him onto a trailer, he would plant his feet and refuse to move. Occasionally, he would start backing up rapidly, but only until he got away from the person tugging at his face. He wasn't being particularly dangerous, but it was super irritating to pay a $30 arena fee and only get to enjoy 10 minutes of riding time because your horse won't leave his home.

It took months of work, and when I say "two steps forward; ten back," I actually mean that literally. Each session, we would creep towards the trailer, sniff the ramp or step up, put a few feet on the trailer, then rapidly back up about 20-30 feet. Then I'd have to, again, coax him towards the trailer, where he would sniff the ramp, and rapidly back up about 20-30 feet.

Now, there are loads of different methods for helping a hard loader realize that the trailer is not to be feared. One involves using a lunge whip on the ground behind the horse to gently urge the horse to move forward. Red, who likes to pick up whips in his own mouth and bang on things that make loud noises in his spare time, decided that a lunge whip was extraordinarily insulting in this situation, so when I tried that method, he reared up and almost landed on my car. That is the perfect example of doing something that should work, but unintentionally escalating the situation.

If you are not willing, able, or excited about having to work on the same scenario/trigger for extended periods of time, with the possibility that you might try something that makes things worse, it is completely rational to call a professional. While adjusting your horse's behavior is the ultimate goal, that goal is not going to be met unless everyone, including the horse, is feeling generally safe and confident.

It turns out, the best way to get Red on a trailer is to pat him, coax him, and have a little grain waiting at the front. He likes to put his front feet in the trailer first in order to feel how his balance is going to change, and then he feels confident hopping in. Unless he's going Home, in which case all I have to say is, "We're going Home, Buddy!" and he leaps in the trailer gleefully. Horses are capable of understanding far more than we realize.

If your horse is doing something pretty straightforward, like rushing past you when you turn them out, or spooking at the flag at the end of the arena, this may be something you can get through with frequent repeated correction. You might need to incorporate some new tools, like a thick pair of leather gloves and a heavy lead rope to stop the rushing. You may also need to try new methods, like lunging your horse day after day in a part of the arena that triggers their flight instincts. Like the Thoroughbred I mentioned earlier, you may find yourself trying everything you can possibly think of.

I strongly recommend to anyone who is experiencing ongoing issues with their horse do all the research they can to figure it out. That may mean typing your horse's exact behavior into a search engine. That may mean reading every book you can on the subject (and thank you for choosing mine as one of your options!). You may obsessively watch videos of professionals working with similarly-minded horses to see what you might be able to use for your own horse. You may also head to the Resources section at the end of this book to help you get started.

My personal recommendation is to do what you can, as you can, and if that doesn't stop the behavior or build communication and trust between you and your horse, then it's a good idea to call a professional. In the meantime, however, keep observing your horse. The more you learn about this peculiar behavior, the more clues you have about the causes and mitigating factors.

Today's smartphones are a fantastic tool for horse folks because we can finally use a pocket-sized device to take a detailed video of our horses that we can then play back, share with others, and use to catalogue different events. Take pictures or videos of your horse misbehaving to see if you can gain even more clues about its triggers and responses.

Yes, a professional should be able to help you diagnose the situation and come up with meaningful ways you and your horse can work through it together, but you see and interact with your horse far more than any other individual. Use this connection–or lack thereof, depending on the behavior–to help guide your methods of behavior adjustment.

And in case I haven't fully made my point about safety, please consider wearing gloves, a helmet, a body protector, and having a helper nearby who can at least dial the phone for an ambulance if necessary. Always put safety first–a rude horse can wait, but even run-of-the-mill injuries can be frustrating for a lifetime.

Chapter 2: When to Call a Professional

Once you've decided you need professional assistance, you need to decide who you're going to call.

As I mentioned in *Why Does My Horse Act Like This: Understanding Equine Behavior in Your New Horse,* the frequent cause for misbehavior is pain or physical discomfort. So, the first professional you may wish to call could be a veterinarian, farrier, chiropractor, or equine dentist. If I had followed my own advice here, I wouldn't have spent weeks trying to get that poor former racehorse to behave in the cross ties when he was trying to tell me that he had open sores on the backs of his ears.

Once your horse is examined, they will either receive a clean bill of health, or the professional will provide you with instructions on how to help your horse become more comfortable. I have seen corrective shoeing and a good dental float work miracles on some cranky horses, so this is always a reasonable path to explore. If you have limited funds for equine interventions, as many of us do, I strongly recommend putting them towards your horse's health and wellness before you start the search for a trainer.

You may also wish to contact a saddle fitter if you notice your horse is acting up only when you ride. In today's society, many of us joke that horses are doing us a favor by allowing us to ride them, so make sure you've got a bit and bridle that fit your horse's mouth and face, and a saddle that fits their back. A saddle fitter can look at the equipment you've been using to ensure it's not the source of discomfort, and help you make adjustments if it is.

You may wish to contact a horse behaviorist for advice. These individuals work almost entirely on the ground, and use their finely-tuned ability to read equine body language in order to get a feel for what they're doing and why. Then, they typically work with the horse for a while to understand what types of reactions they have, when they have them, why they have them, and what works best to get their attention and keep it. Most equine behavior experts will work with your horse to create pressure, and gauge how they work with you and communicate their needs. As a result, you'll have professional insight into your horse's behavior, as well as tips and tools for increasing your equine communication skills.

A trainer's role is typically very similar in that they will work with your horse and evaluate its behavior. However, while a behavior specialist's goal is to open up communication to avoid evasive behavior, a trainer will generally put a stop to the horse's bad manners and teach them how to "act right."

You may hear of some equine professionals referred to as "cowboys." While this frequently refers to actual professionals who work with cattle, horses, and livestock, there may be times when you hear the term out of that context. Generally speaking, these cowboys are folks who aren't full-time trainers, but they volunteer to do the dirty work when it comes to breaking out a horse. They've earned their title due to being able to jump on, stay on, and safely eject themselves from very green horses who do not warm up to the idea of saddle training. Trainers often hire cowboys to work with them to help them with the really dangerous stuff. Occasionally, cowboys will hang out their own shingle as a trainer and accept some projects that they feel will help them build their credentials. Though the term is often associated with the type of trainer who will use "quick fixes" and potentially harsh treatment, that's not always the case. Anyone who works with your horse should be vetted for suitability, regardless of their job title.

When horses are put in training, it's typically for months at a time. Trainers will frequently put 30, 60, or 90 days of training on a particular beast. The length of time a horse spends with a trainer usually depends on how much the horse's owner wants said beast to learn, and how willing the horse is to learn. Your horse may stay at the trainer's facility for this time period—which means you'll have to pay board—or your trainer may elect to come to your horse's location a certain number of times each week.

Trainers rarely work on just one issue, unless it's a thoroughly compounded and deep-rooted issue. Horses who have been deeply traumatized, for example, will typically have a few different triggers to deal with, which can pop up in a variety of situations. You may not even be aware of how sincere your horse is about their feelings on a particular matter because once that instinct kicks in, things escalate quickly. Therefore, a trainer will work towards a particular goal, and help kick any other triggers, habits, or aggressions that might be stirred up throughout the process.

Trainers can also help us, the horse's person, work through any triggers, habits, or aggressiveness that we might display, as well. Since your horse is constantly gauging your body language and communication as well, it is possible that you're accidentally telling your horse that everything is terrible and they need to be on high alert. Knowing how to act, what to do, and how to respond to your horse's flights of fancy can help you feel more confident in working with your horse on a daily basis.

Finding a trainer can be an involved process, however. In *Why Does My Horse Act Like This: Understanding Equine Behavior in your New Horse,* we discussed the qualities to look for in a trainer. Again, I don't want to be too repetitive, but I strongly recommend:

- Meeting the trainer in person
- Touring their facility and meeting their personal horses
- Bringing them to where your horse lives to get a feel for their daily life and routine
- Watching them work
- Asking for references and following up to get these individuals' take on the trainer's abilities
- Asking trusted professionals in your area what they think of this trainer
- Sharing the information you've received from your vet, farrier, chiropractor, etc. when coming up with a training plan

You may also ask if you can be present when the trainer works with your horse, as possible given your schedule. I personally find it very suspicious if a trainer says I cannot be there, though there are some scenarios wherein it's a good idea for the trainer to work with a horse alone. For example, your trainer may want to see if your horse's behavior is replicated when you aren't around. On the whole, though, your trainer should encourage you to participate in your horse's growth and development so that you can help your horse maintain their good manners.

Another neat thing most people don't realize is that you can pull your horse from training. Depending on the contract you sign (and you should always sign a contract detailing expectations, time frames, and expenses), you may forfeit your payment by doing this. However, if you feel your horse is not responding to your trainer's methodology, or you feel uncomfortable with the process, you may wish to pursue this opportunity.

Ultimately, the intervention of a professional should help you feel more confident and understanding of your horse's particular issues. While the opinion of equine professionals will rarely cause your horse's behavior to change immediately, the goal of all professionals should be to work with you and your horse within your means and ability to help find harmony. That will likely mean change and compromise for you and your horse, but that's really what building a relationship with a horse is. Learning how to work with each other and communicate effectively is really the best part of sharing our lives with our equine companions. At least, that's my take on it!

Chapter 3: When to Give Up – and How

There seems to be this general idea that once you choose to share your life with a horse, there's no getting out of it. It is true that many of us become strongly bonded to our horses and choose to move heaven and Earth to ensure that we're able to live together for as long as possible. Most behavioral issues are a mere hiccup or blip in the overall relationship, and once communication has been established and attitudes adjusted all around, that wonderful relationship resumes.

But just because that's the norm doesn't mean it ends up that way every time. You may find that your horse's behavioral issues are more than you can handle. You may become very frightened of your horse, which can escalate the situation until it spirals far out of your control. You may wonder why you're spending half of your paycheck on an animal you can't stand to be around. You may have been injured or traumatized by your horse's actions, and are physically unable to take matters into your own hands. Trainers can be expensive, and you may not be able to swing the extra cost. Or, the stark reality may dawn on you that you and this creature are simply not meant to be friends.

Many people feel that adopting an animal of any species and bringing them into your home means you're signing on to care for them until the very end. That is true, but while some people define "the end" as "the end of life" for either pet or person, my years in equine rescue and training have taught me that it's best to consider it "the end of the partnership."

It could very well be that you and your horse are simply ill-suited for each other. Whether you have a personality clash, or they aren't comfortable in the living situation you are able to provide for them, it is ok to admit that this is simply not the horse for you. It is **not** ok to pretend like nothing is happening and wait for the problem to go away on its own.

When I worked at a rescue facility, we would frequently have our stalls filled with emaciated horses with skin sores and overgrown hooves at the end of the year. When the sun came out and the weather turned nice, well-intentioned folks would decide to follow their dreams of owning a horse. But once the horse began to act in a way the new owners couldn't handle, these folks became frightened of the horse. Instead of doing anything about it right away, they would neglect the horse. They were too terrified to bring them in from the field, or go into their stalls to feed them, or interact with them in any way.

Horses have a strong survival instinct, so they tend to find ways to survive. But the less you communicate with your horse, the less the horse will return the favor. Instead of leaning on their established knowledge, they'll revert back to feral horse ways, working on staying alive over greeting humans with a friendly nicker and being polite.

As a result, these well-meaning people would be embarrassed at their perceived failure, ignore the horses until the guilt was too great, and then have no idea what to do with them. Since the horses were lame and unhealthy due to lack of care, they would bring them to the rescue. You see, all of those big fancy barns with gleaming horses and loving, careful humans aren't in the market for skinny horses who will need thousands of dollars in vet and farrier work in order to be sound and happy again. Once your neglect—however well-meaning you thought you were–has impacted your horse's health, the number of safe, kind, happy homes you can find for that horse have dropped sharply.

Therefore, I strongly encourage everyone to take care of their horses (and all other animals) with the absolute best standard of care until the end of your relationship. If you find that you cannot establish the right relationship with your horse, start looking for a new home immediately. The longer you wait to find your horse a home, the lesser chance you have of that being a fantastic home where your horse will thrive.

Here's my recommended approach for this process:

Step 1: Contact the former owner if possible. Explain what the horse is doing, and ask kindly if that's a new behavior, or something they've observed in the past. You may be surprised at how much information wasn't mentioned at the time of purchase. Imagine my shock when I described what Belle was doing to her former owner, and she replied, "Oh, haven't you been giving her an ulcer supplement?"

I also recommend having the difficult "what if this doesn't work out?" conversation during the purchase process. Not all folks are willing or able to take back a horse they've sold, but they may also have resources you can connect with to potentially rehome your horse. Each time I've sold a horse, I've included all of my contact information (email, and phone), as well as the name of a local rescue I trust. I do not guarantee that I can actively take the horse back, but that I am willing to do my best to help them find a new home for the horse if they would like the assistance.

All of this being said, it's important to remember that the horse's former owner sold them for a reason–because they were no longer willing or able to care for them. Once you have paid for the horse and signed the bill of sale (always get a bill of sale), the former owner rarely has any legal obligations towards you and the horse. Therefore it is possible that this path may not be lucrative, or even available to you. That's when we move to Step 2.

Step 2: At this point, you might consider contacting local trainers, cowboys, and lesson barns to see if they are in need of a project horse. Be transparent about why you are not keeping the horse.

A "project horse" is one who needs some work before they're fully considered an Equine Good Citizen. They may be very green, have some bad habits, or just need to get back into consistent work after an extended time off due to illness, injury, or any other reason. A project horse who does not need to be completely rehabilitated is a diamond in the rough, and many trainers, cowboys, or lesson barns with a bevy of experienced amateurs looking to bring up their own horse will jump on the opportunity to obtain a healthy horse, even if it does come with a few "idiosyncrasies."

If your horse is a decent being when at work, you might contact a local chapter of 4H or the United States Pony Club to see if they have any members who might be a good fit for your horse. I actually managed to rehome a horse who was not a good fit for me through Pony Club members networking across the country to find the perfect family for him.

You may also wish to speak with your vet, farrier, chiropractor, feed supplier, and other equine or farm-related professionals in your area. They may also know someone looking for a horse just like yours.

Years ago, I was leasing Red to a friend who lived on the other side of the state. When the lease was coming to an end, I was struggling to find a place to put him for the time being. Amazingly enough, a very nice lady who ran an equine therapy facility stopped in to grab a bottle from the winery where I worked. She was the only customer, so we started talking. A few weeks later, she was Red's new lessee, and she loved having him around until her lease ended. Reach out to anyone you can think of who might know someone who knows someone!

Step 3: Post sales information everywhere you can online. Some social media platforms allow for horse sales groups and sales ads, but not all of them, so check the rules to avoid getting yourself banned.

There are many online sales websites for horses, and I've linked a few in the Resources section. Proceed with caution because it's very easy to find and fall in love with a horse via these sites– that's how I found Red! Some may offer free options for advertising a horse for sale, while others involve a fee or commission. Check the details before you get started.

Step 4: If you are getting to the point where you don't think anyone will take your horse, it's time to call a rescue. Explain that you are surrendering your horse, and be honest about the problems you've had. The first rescue may not be able to take your horse, but they should be able to help you find additional resources to reach out to. You may also be invited to check out the rescue facility to get a feel for the care they will provide for your horse. Many rescues in the United States are private 501(c) (3) organizations, which means they're funded by donations and run by volunteers. As a result, some rescues are gorgeous and immaculate, while others are fueled by a bunch of horse-crazy volunteers shoveling manure and administering medication between conference calls, Zoom meetings, and school obligations.

Another common question I get is "how do you make sure you get your money back when you sell a horse." You do not. There is rarely a positive return on investment or ROI on a horse. Grand Prix and Masters level performance horses, racehorses, and horses who break into the show business are some of the only horses I know who have come close to recouping their overall cost. Horses cost a lot–mentally, physically, emotionally, and monetarily.

Furthermore, the horse market changes a lot. In 2008, horses became very inexpensive, thanks to the financial events of the year and drop in equine sports participation. I worked at the rescue then, and our stalls were packed with horses who were relatively healthy and needed a minor tune-up in order to be productive beasts. Their owners had simply lost their jobs and couldn't afford them any longer. The average monthly cost per horse at that particular facility, at that specific point in time, was about $275. We were adopting the horses out at $100 each. No ROI here!

So, if you are frustrated by someone "low-balling" you on the purchase of your horse, you will need to consider which is more important to you: the money, or knowing your horse is likely going to a decent home. Either option is valid–I cannot judge someone for wanting the money they need to keep a roof over the head and meals in their bellies–but remember, a horse who is not being fed, cared for, and trained properly will be harder to rehome. The faster your horse is sold or placed, the more immediate the financial impact of the sale, too.

That being said, if a good home for your horse is important to you, feel empowered to ask questions of any potential buyer to get a feel for their standards of care and the type of home your horse will have going forward. Your horse is your responsibility until the bill of sale is signed and they are transported to their new home.

Whichever path you choose, know that your choice is valid, as are all the feelings you have about your decision. While I consider myself an experienced horse person, I have hired trainers to help me in areas where I lacked experience and learned a lot in the process. A good trainer can really help open up communication between a human and a horse, which can make an already good relationship phenomenal.

I have also had to rehome a horse, as I mentioned earlier. It was a very difficult decision, based on my life situation at the time. The main consideration was that I had injured my spine, and I couldn't work with him in a way that he needed to be worked with. I attempted to find a leasing home for him, but ultimately, he went to a family in another state who rode him daily, took weekly lessons with him, and went trail riding with him several times a week. It was perfect for him, and I love getting photo updates of his shenanigans.

It is entirely up to you how you choose to deal with your horse's behavioral issues. Please be aware that they will not resolve themselves. Your horse will still need to be fed, watered, and cared for. The more you handle your horse, the more opportunities you have to establish communication with them. In turn, that gives you a greater chance of working out the problematic behavior, if you choose to do so. Just be sure to keep everyone's safety in mind, and know that it is not shameful to look for help.

If you choose to look for help, take the time to get the right helper for you and your horse. Whether that's someone who can help you support your horse physically–like a vet–or a behaviorist or trainer, you're looking for someone who can help you and your horse. Your goal is to learn and grow as a horse person, while your professional's goal is to identify the source of the behavior and help the horse understand why it's inappropriate.

But sometimes, there are issues between a horse and their human that even the best of trainers can't resolve. Have you ever met a person and thought you might become friends, only to discover after hanging out a few times that you didn't enjoy each other's presence that much? You can't train away that lack of chemistry. You also can't train away money issues or find a magic supplement to feed your horse that will quell your fears.

When you purchased your horse, you signed on to be responsible for their well-being until the end of your relationship. That relationship may change. Just make sure you choose the most responsible path for your horse and yourself.

SECTION FIVE: THE GREAT DE-BATES

As you search for possible solutions to your horse's puzzling behavior, you will find that there are many different training and communication methods. You will also find that horse people either accept that there are many potential tools to add to the horse training toolbox, or they vehemently and exhaustively oppose or uphold specific methods. There are those who swear by Pat Parelli's horsemanship methods, those who view them as some sort of bizarre joke, and those who view some of his theories as helpful, but not necessarily all of it.

I personally do not make judgements on a trainer's methods until I get a feel for their process. I also believe that no two horses will respond exactly the same to the same training methods. This is also true of humans–it's simply not reasonable to expect two people to learn and work identically. I believe that if we get locked into a method, program, or theory without exploring other possibilities, we're doing a great injustice to our horses and ourselves. We can't learn and grow unless we quite literally step out of our comfort zones to appreciate and understand new information.

That being said, there are some training methods and theories that I find more dangerous than effective. You'll find that most horse people have a pretty firm stance towards things they feel are abusive versus potentially beneficial. Similarly, some people have indelible opinions about rewarding horses. Ultimately, no training is cruel, dangerous, or abusive unless it is taken past the regard for the long-term well-being of the horse and human.

To illustrate this point, I'd like to discuss a couple of the most popular debates of equine training and building good manners. These are not black and white issues; in fact, there are many "if/then" or "yes, but" statements that can be issued in either debate. I'll present the facts with as little bias as possible to allow you to make your decisions.

Debate 1 - Quick Fixes: Efficient or Dangerous?

Horse people are known for their bizarre and genius uses for simple and common items, like duct tape and baling twine. We like quick fixes because we like it when things are immediately taken care of at the least possible expense. That allows us to move more quickly onto the next disaster. There is no lack of disasters for horse people. Whether the fence is coming down, the insulation is being chewed up by the birds, or raccoons have figured out how to get in the feed room again, something always needs our attention. Throw in our natural human appreciation for immediate gratification, and the "quick and easy" way may seem very tempting.

Often in the horse world, "quick and easy" involves tools that teach horses not to do a certain thing by providing pain or pressure when they do that exact thing. Hobbles are used to bind a horse's rear legs together so that if they feel inclined to buck or kick, they'll be unable to land on their feet. Draw reins put pressure on a horse's mouth when they raise their head, encouraging them to release their necks downwards. Side reins have a similar purpose, but are used when a horse is not being ridden, which means they're fighting the pressure they're inflicting on themselves. Certain bits create discomfort on the bars of a horse's mouth or tongue to prevent them from ignoring their rider's hands. Stud chains create pressure across a horse's nose and face to make raising their heads uncomfortable.

Other tools are used to create performance. Some gaited horses wear padding and chains that encourage them to exaggerate their natural gaits. Certain breeds of horses with a naturally high-set tail will be shown with skin irritants applied to the underside of the dock to cause the horse to hold their tails even higher. Spurs and crops are used as an extension of a rider's leg to request more hind leg action from a horse under saddle.

Most of these tools are not harmful in theory, but can be in practice. A horse left in their stall in hobbles can damage themselves if they land in a strange position or get stuck by a wall with no way to get up. Draw reins, side reins, and training bits in harsh and impatient hands can damage a horse's neck and mouth as they fight the pressure. Horses have been known to react dramatically to this type of pressure by rearing and flipping backwards to escape. These actions can be fatal to both horse and human. Light padding can be beneficial and even therapeutic, but heavy padding can impact the shape and movement of a horse's muscles, tendons, and ligaments over time. Using spurs and crops too much can tell a horse that they don't need to respond to more subtle commands, while possibly causing skin injury if used injudiciously.

Additionally, we have to take into consideration whether we really want to cause our horses pain. Momentary discomfort and pressure is one thing, but extended periods of being asked to do something that is beyond the horse's natural capability is different. Most horses respond to pressure instantly. However, that response may be to stop, look at you, and listen to what you are trying to communicate, or it may be to react even more defensively. Worst of all, you don't know what reaction a horse may have until you try, which can potentially mean you have one shot to either train or traumatize the horse with these tools.

There are horse people who believe in, and are physically and mentally capable of continuing, the escalation process with a horse until the horse gives up. There are trainers who are willing to trip and flip horses to assert dominance, or who will wrestle horses to the ground to demonstrate why they want to consider this human their leader. There are also trainers who believe that encouraging a horse to fear them is a good way to prevent aggressive behavior from the horse. The theory behind these training processes is the natural pecking order found in horse herds. Horses physically duke it out in order to assert dominance over their herd members, both in the wild and in the pasture. If a human exerts physical dominance over a horse, then clearly that horse will think of that human as the head of the herd. The faster this is done, the more quickly the trainer can move forward with the horse's progress.

The trainers who employ quick fixes, like harsh or exaggerated use of tools, or using fear and pain as motivators argue that these methods are not only faster, since they drive home the point immediately, but more effective in the long run, because the horse learns to not argue with the human from the onset. This means that more meaningful training is more immediate. For example, if a horse is intended to hit the show circuit in time for the Nationals, they need to knock off the attitude and nasty behavior immediately so they can focus on the skills necessary to help them succeed in the show circuit. In other cases, a trainer will intentionally attempt to "break a horse's spirit" so that they can be safe in any situation, with any rider, and hopefully never act out.

Others feel that this method of exerting dominance over a horse is too much, too quickly. Following the "Ask, Tell, Demand" principles of horsemanship, a trainer should escalate from the lightest request for an action to the harshest insistence over a period of time, giving the horse the opportunity to process and respond to the request. Horses can pick up and react to even the most minute changes in body language, so why stress them out with physical and mental pain when a simple change in how you stand in relation to the horse can accomplish the same result over time and with repetition?

Like the great debate over spanking children in the human world, there are a lot of "yes, but" statements in between both sides. For example, some people believe that hitting a horse harshly with a whip as a form of defense (such as if a horse is charging towards you) is acceptable, as long as it is not used consistently. There are many arguments for how any training method can be cruel if done improperly, and any training method could also be considered a safety measure, if used appropriately.

At the same time, many people agree that there is no such thing as "common" usage of tools and quick fix training techniques, too. That is, there are ways to use these tools and techniques inadequately, effectively, or inhumanely. But remember that horses, like toddlers, all have a different outlook towards and tolerance for change, both of which can be unpredictable. What one horse tolerates well might be a terrible traumatic event to another horse. And, when you take into account that humans may act differently each day, depending on their mood, how they slept, what they've eaten, or how things are going so far that day, it is possible to be harsher with tools and techniques than consciously intended.

Quick fixes are generally effective, and the "quick" part is not often a misnomer. But the potential for injury is high, and there are some horses who will fight against these methods literally, and sadly, to the death. Improperly used tools and techniques can result in spinal, skeletal, and structural damage that may be irreversible due to the fast and extreme way a horse's body may be conditioned. Other injuries, such as cuts and lacerations, will likely heal, though scarring is a concern, especially if you plan to take a horse into the show pen.

As a horse owner, it is up to you to determine how forceful you get with your horse's training. Whether that's using these tools and techniques yourself, or hiring a trainer who will use these methods on your horse, it is up to you to observe and decide how well your horse is tolerating them, and whether you are comfortable with the process and the results.

Debate 2 - To Treat or Not to Treat?

If you're wondering how treats could possibly be considered a bad thing, you're not alone. Everyone loves treats, right? That's actually the problem. Some horses really love treats–to the point where they'll become aggressive about them.

Horses have large teeth that are designed for grinding roughage all day. They can, do, and will use their mouth, lips, and teeth to communicate all sorts of messages, including pleasure and pain. Sometimes, that includes biting. While a horse lightly nipping at another horse is generally their way of saying, "Hey buddy–watch out!," that same light nip might cause a nasty bruise or open wound on our thin human skin. Therefore, it's important that we teach our horses that they need to keep their mouths to themselves when humans are involved and choose another form of communication.

Yet, in the same breath, we also place a flat palm full of treats under a horse's nose and expect them to gingerly use their lips and tongue to retrieve them. Most horses have no problem with this, but some horses can get really nasty about this, aggressively snapping at humans whenever they want to be left alone, fed, or are bored.

Some trainers feel that there is a direct correlation between hand feeding treats and increased aggressive biting behavior. Some feel that the validity of this potential link really depends on the horse, their lifestyle, and any changes in their lives. Some feel that this is all a bunch of bunk, and that treats are the best way to train a horse.

In a training scenario, a horse is typically offered a treat as incentive for doing something "good," like walking towards the trainer, stretching its neck and back, or allowing the trainer to touch them in a ticklish or uncomfortable place. Occasionally, horses are offered treats as a distraction, just as you might offer a toddler a lollipop while they're getting a shot at the doctor's office.

The most common time a horse is offered treats is at the end of a work session. Many riders, drivers, and handlers praise their horses after a particularly enjoyable and educational practice with a handful of treats.

Anything your horse likes to eat can be considered a treat. Apples and carrots are some of the more well-known options, but there are many different types of equine yummies to choose from. Some feed companies will make treats that address a certain issue, providing probiotics for gastric support or joint supplements for reducing pain and inflammation. Some treats provide supplemental nutrition, like extra beet pulp and fiber to aid in digestion and weight maintenance.

Some people extend the "apples and carrots" scenario a bit further to "anything they happen to have handy," including sandwiches, soda, candy, and salty treats. Not all human food is intended to be eaten by horses, though. Chocolate is toxic to horses, and bread products can swell in the horse's esophagus and lead to a choke episode. Since horses can colic after eating the same meal every day, you may or may not feel comfortable finding out first hand where your horse's tolerance level for human food is.

Many equestrians feel that the occasional treat tossed in the horse's feed bucket isn't a big deal. After all, humans tend to snack after a good workout, too.

On the other hand, there are those who feel that a horse should receive positive reinforcement at the moment they are demonstrating good behavior. That may mean interrupting a ride or work session to distribute treats and praise. Opponents of treats feel there are different ways to offer your horse a reward for good performance, including vocal cues, like, "good pony!" spoken in an enthusiastic, warm voice, or offering a pat or scratch along your horse's neck or withers if you're mounted. They feel that horses will learn to stop what they're doing to demand a treat any time they perform a task for which they've been rewarded in the past.

Many feel that a "pressure and release" system is more than adequate for explaining certain situations to horses. If a horse is raising their head and pulling on the lead rope when you're escorting them from paddock to stall, for example, many feel that the best way to teach a horse that this is unacceptable is to add a heavier lead rope or stud chain that will put extra pressure on a horse's face. When they stop pulling, the pressure releases, and the handler or trainer can give the horse pats and verbal praise. Others feel that the point is not fully reinforced unless an incentive like a treat is offered. Some believe that giving a horse treats will make them more eager to perform correctly for their trainer or handler the first time.

Additional arguments against treats state that the added calories can cause weight gain and lead to insulin resistance, much as overindulging in food as a human has been found to correlate with an increase in health risks. Some feel that giving a horse too many treats is similar to giving a toddler too many sweets—while it may coax the desired behavior out of them, it can lead to an increased dependence on a less nutritional source of energy. Moderation and appropriate levels of exercise can mitigate these potential issues.

You will have to evaluate for yourself whether you think that treats are likely to turn your horse into a demanding, biting monster. You may choose to give your horses treats after a positive work session, at random, or whenever they do what you want them to do. You may decide that your horse can be trained to accept treats by hand, or insist that treats are only provided in a safe feed dish. If you decide to allow treats, many people feel that it's important to monitor the amount, type, frequency, and delivery method of treats to ensure anyone who interacts with your horse respects these wishes.

As you explore training methods, experts, and opportunities, you will likely encounter some of the strong opinions on either side of these great debates. I encourage you to consider all sides and opinions, and bear in mind that every horse is different.

Furthermore, I encourage you to keep an open mind and consider your own personal horse's behaviors and preferences when exploring different methods and techniques for dealing with inappropriate behavior in your horse. You are your horse's advocate. You are their voice, and you can tell a professional what you will and will not allow them to do with your horse. If you are boarding, make sure your barn owner and staff know your preferences so they can respect them as well.

We all come from different backgrounds and experiences, just like our horses. When confronted with new training styles and mechanics, I encourage you to listen and get a feel for what's really being done before you decide whether or not that is a method that you support or advocate for your own horse.

CONCLUSION

So there you go: The secret to a well-mannered horse is lots of patience, observation, and making good choices! That may sound simple, but you might also discover that being a horse person is a lot more involved than you thought.

If your horse starts acting strangely seemingly overnight, I strongly urge you to call your vet first and foremost. Horses don't typically change personalities or develop bad habits immediately. There may be something physically inspiring this dramatic shift in attitude.

But, if your horse has always been a grumpy old cuss who tries to bite during the grooming and tacking up process, that might just be established habits shining through. Many horses learn quickly that doing something drastic results in them getting exactly what they want, which is often "to be left alone eating grass and dozing in the sun."

Your horse may also be relying on their senses and instincts to tell them what's good and what's dangerous. Even the most well-trained horses can react to something that's strange to them. As part of your deal to be responsible for your horse's well-being, you are tasked with helping your horse understand that their reaction is inappropriate, and guide them towards making better choices.

You don't, however, have to do that alone. Asking for help from a medical or training professional can be beneficial for your growth as a horse person, and your horse's growth as a well-mannered equine. And, in some cases, you may need to evaluate if this is the right horse for you, and the right home for your horse.

You may have noticed that I don't mention a lot of specific training methods or provide a lot of "how-to" information. I've received a few inquiries about that, and I'm not trying to hold out on amazing miracle-working magic. I try not to mention a lot of detail about horse training because I very much don't want someone to try my methods on their own horses, have it fail miserably for any reason, and feel like I have personally done something terrible to your horse.

Horse training includes a lot of observation, analysis, trying things, finding out they don't work, re-evaluating the situation, trying something different, and repeating all of these steps until something clicks and you and your horse are both on the same page. Sometimes this process takes 30 days, and sometimes you have less than 30 seconds to make a decision because a horse is about to go bonkers. The timing of both reward and punishment, or positive and negative reinforcement, or pressure and release is imperative to training success. If you miss an opportunity, you have to wait until the stars align to recreate that moment. You can't force a horse to understand, there is no magic wand, and undoing a behavior that a horse has been doing for years may take just as long.

If I can't see your horse or learn from you what your horse is doing, I simply don't feel comfortable providing training advice. The area between "learning" and "making things worse" is simply too wide and too grey for me to blindly recommend an umbrella course of action through a book. There are things I have done with Red that would make a huge mess with Belle. Horses are just too different for everything to work perfectly the first time.

I recommend checking out some of the training sites in the Resources section to see which methods might jive best with you and your horse's personalities. Don't just watch one video from each trainer–binge watch as many videos as you can! You may feel inspired to try some of the things you see in the videos with your horse, and I encourage it, as long as you feel safe and comfortable and do not take any unnecessary risks. If you are scared, skip it and go back to doing something familiar. You are not a failure. You are choosing the well-being of yourself and your horse.

A perfectly-behaved horse is hard to come by. I have never met a horse who was completely and utterly "bomb proof," as we say. There are horses who are more laid back about their surroundings, like Red. There are horses who don't mind the activities occurring around them, as long as they aren't asked to do anything they don't want to do, like Belle. And there are horses for whom everything is new, exciting, and potentially dangerous. Like any other living being, horses can be a little different from day to day. Observing them carefully every day can help you decide which of their behaviors are learned, which are reactions that need redirected, and which may be signs that something's not quite right, or, "NQR" as my vet says.

I wish you all the best as you work with your equine buddy. I hope you have the patience you need to observe and understand the situation, the serenity to objectively make decisions for next steps, and the clarity to know when you need to back off or get help. Horses are big, powerful, scary...and wonderful, majestic, and cuddly. Any conversation you have with your horse about manners is going to take time, and you may have to repeat yourself a few times over the years. But, just like raising a child through those wildly unpredictable toddler years, those positive aspects of the relationship often shine through.

I hope this book and the resources that follow are helpful to you as you continue your journey with your horse. I wish you many fulfilling years in your partnership, with a few nips and "NO!"s, and plenty of pats and praise!

RESOURCES

While I love sharing my knowledge and experiences with friends and readers, I recognize that I am not the final or only word when it comes to equine behavior, communication, or training. Therefore, I like to include a variety of perspectives on these topics.

I consider each of the following resources credible and worthy of reading and reflecting upon, but I also want to make it clear that I have no association with any of the people, websites, studies, resources, or entities included below. I don't want this to be construed as support, advocacy, or even agreement with any of the opinions discussed in these resources. This is merely a collection of links to publicly available websites and videos that help explain or demonstrate the points we've discussed in greater detail.

Since I can't answer every question you may have along the way, I thought it would be helpful to provide some very thorough resources! Click through with an open mind, and feel free to explore some of the publications or websites linked as well—many include a wealth of knowledge on a variety of topics.

Print Articles, PDFs, and Blogs

Lifestyle and Behavior Correlations

While I've covered this topic in a different book, the connection between a horse's behavior and their contentment with their daily life is undeniable. These links lead to resources that can help you understand why your horse may be responding and reacting in certain ways, based on how they live.

Equus Magazine, "Are you setting your horse up for bad behavior?: https://equusmagazine.com/behavior/how-management-affects-behavior/

Horse and Rider blog, "4 Reasons Why Your Horse Is Too Hot to Handle" https://horseandrider.com/blog/horse-too-hot-to-handle-anxious-nervous/

National Park Service (NPS) guide, "Wild Horse Behavior" https://www.nps.gov/calo/learn/nature/up-load/2007-Wild-Horse-Behavior.pdf

Nervous Behavior

The following resources may help those who are new to horses to better understand horse behavior. Each link focuses specifically on nervous behavior, which may help you better identify when your horse is being a brat, and when they are genuinely concerned.

Equus Magazine, "Do's and Don'ts in dealing with a nervous horse" https://equusmagazine.com/behavior/dealing-with-a-nervous-horse/

Equine Helper, "Signs a Horse Is Anxious, Nervous, or Stressed"
https://equinehelper.com/signs-a-horse-is-stressed/

Horse Journals, "The Anxious Horse: Working Through Tension"
https://www.horsejournals.com/riding-training/general/schooling/anxious-horse-working-through-tension

Facial Expressions

Being able to read and understand your horse's facial expressions can be very helpful when understanding why they're acting out. These resources can help you better identify what your horse is thinking or feeling, based on their expressions and movement.

CNN.com, "Horses can make facial expressions just like humans"
https://www.cnn.com/2018/06/26/sport/horse-facial-expressions-spt/index.html

PLOS One research article, "Development and validation of the facial scale (FaceSed) to evaluate sedation in horses"
https://journals.plos.org/plosone/article?id=10.1371/journal.pone.0251909

The Hoof Blog, "Sue Dyson: Double video explanation of equine ethogram for recognizing lameness and pain"
https://hoofcare.blogspot.com/2017/06/sue-dyson-equine-ethogram-facial-expression-lameness-video.html

Similarly, a horse's body language can tell us a lot about where a horse is both mentally and emotionally. These articles help identify and demonstrate the potential meaning behind different body movements and positioning.

Horse Illustrated magazine, "Equine Body Language"
https://www.horseillustrated.com/horse-keeping-horse-body-language

Horse Illustrated magazine, "How to Speak Horse"
https://www.horseillustrated.com/horse-keeping-how-to-speak-horse

Equine Wellness magazine, "Top 10 equine body language postures"
https://equinewellnessmagazine.com/top-10-body-language-postures/

Equine Spot website, "Understand Horse Body Language and You'll Unlock the Equine Communication Code"
https://www.equinespot.com/horse-body-language.html

Equus magazine, "What Your Horse's Tail Tells You"
https://equusmagazine.com/horse-care/horsetail_062206/

Horse Network, "Say What? A Quick Guide to Decoding Your Horse's Body Language"
https://horsenetwork.com/2017/05/say-what-a-quick-guide-to-decoding-your-horse-s-body-language/

Finding a Trainer

Finding a trainer can be a daunting task, no matter how many times you've successfully searched for one in the past. These sites offer some tips for finding, connecting with, and evaluating a trainer for your horse.

American Quarter Horse Association, "Find a Professional"
https://www.aqha.com/find-a-trainer1

Success Under Saddle Coaching, "How to Find an Exceptional Horse Trainer, Riding Instructor or Coach"
https://successundersaddle.com/how-to-find-an-exceptional-horse-trainer-riding-instructor-coach/

The Horse website, "Finding a Horse Trainer Who's Right for You (Or Your Child)"
https://thehorse.com/167813/finding-a-horse-trainer-whos-right-for-you/

Horse and Rider magazine, " How (and Why) to Find a Trainer"
https://horseandrider.com/western-horse-training-tips/find-trainer-25708/

Horse Sales Sites

I strongly recommend exercising extreme willpower when perusing sales ads!

Equine.com
https://www.equine.com/

Dreamhorse.com

https://www.dreamhorse.com/

Horseclicks.com

https://www.horseclicks.com/
Foods That Horses Shouldn't Eat

For those who are curious about what "people food" horses can and cannot eat, these sites help explain the whats and whys.

Saddlebox gifts, "What Foods & Plants are Poisonous to Horses?"

https://www.saddlebox.net/what-foods-plants-are-poisonous-to-horses/

Horse Fact Book blog, "What Foods & Plants Are Harmful To Horses? 25 Things They Should NEVER Eat"

https://www.horsefactbook.com/guides/what-horses-should-never-eat/

Training Tools and How They Work

Some of the training tools mentioned throughout this book may be new to you, so I've included a few links to articles and a video that can help explain these tools and how they can be used to educate and inform a horse about their behavior.

US Whip product blog, "A Guide to Horse Training Tools, Whips, Crops"

https://uswhip.com/blog/a-guide-to-horse-training-tools-whips-crops/

Horse Journals magazine, "The Science of Tack and Training Aids" https://www.horsejournals.com/riding-training/tack-gear/english/science-tack-and-training-aids

Thehorse.com, "Training Aid Fact and Fiction for Better Riding"
https://thehorse.com/182591/training-aid-fact-and-fiction-for-better-riding/

Video: Larry Trocha, "Horse Training Aids: What they are & why use them"
https://www.youtube.com/watch?v=5RecmGz0Vss

Videos

Facial Expressions and Body Language

If you prefer a more detailed and largely visual exploration of how horses try to communicate with us, consider watching these videos. They may help you gain greater insight and appreciation for the subtleties of equine body language.

EquineHelper Channel, "READING HORSE BODY LANGUAGE AND BEHAVIOR" https://www.youtube.com/watch?v=l95J-kS7M0U

Spalding Labs Channel, "10 Equine Behaviors Explained by Dr. Robert M. Miller"
https://www.youtube.com/watch?v=bUiTv-ZzthQ

Mustang Maddy Channel, "How to Read Your Horse's Emotions"
https://www.youtube.com/watch?v=DSFfpmg1iR0

The following professionals are well-known trainers with established methods, theories, and procedures. Remember that I'm not specifically agreeing with or advocating for any of these trainers, but I hope to present you with several different perspectives on training and behavioral issues. I encourage you to watch as many of these as you like to get a feel for all of the different tools and opportunities that exist to help your horse become a good citizen!

Monty Roberts - https://www.youtube.com/watch?v=smN9yebcibc

Clinton Anderson - https://www.youtube.com/watch?v=vZRLA7lvh7Q

Pat Parelli - https://www.youtube.com/watch?v=aAFKxsjpyoY

Linda Tellington-Jones - https://www.youtube.com/watch?v=h9svZD5UKG4

John Lyons - https://www.youtube.com/watch?v=zXGLMEpXAr0

Warwick Schiller - https://www.youtube.com/watch?v=qincEZod6mQ

West Taylor - https://www.youtube.com/watch?v=bQag2hHFHq0

Sam VanFleet - https://www.youtube.com/watch?v=5JyJ7ybG0fU

LEAVE A REVIEW ON AMAZON:

Reviews and feedback help improve this book and the author. If you enjoy this book, we would greatly appreciate it if you could take a few moments to share your opinion and post a review on Amazon.

ALSO BY MEREDITH HILL

Before Your Horse Comes Home

Finding Your First Horse

I Have A Horse... Now What?

Why Does My Horse Act like this?